The Gospel According to Thomas

The Ultimate Revelation

Other Writings by the Author

These and other books
Available through:
Mystics of the World
Eliot, Maine
www.mysticsoftheworld.com

The Gospel According to Thomas

The Ultimate Revelation

Marie S. Watts

The Gospel According to Thomas

Mystics of the World First Edition 2015
Published by Mystics of the World
ISBN-13:9780692407707
ISBN-10:0692407707

For information contact:
Mystics of the World
Eliot, Maine
www.mysticsoftheworld.com

Cover graphics by Margra Muirhead
Printed by CreateSpace
Available from Mystics of the World
and Amazon.com

৶ ৶

Marie S. Watts

To Noel Andrews
with love and gratitude

Contents

*The author lovingly
dedicates this book to YOU, the Reader.*

Introduction

It is with great joy and humility that I share the revelations of these words of Jesus with you— "joy" because only in the spiritual significance of these words can we know God and, knowing God, know ourselves; "humility" because only God could reveal such glorious truths.

The beauty of *The Gospel According to Thomas* is that it is absolutely authentic. The text has not been altered or changed, and it is just the words as they were spoken by the one called Jesus.

Needless to say, this is an entirely spiritual interpretation of this Gospel. It would be impossible to interpret this beautiful text intellectually. As we know, that which is called a human mind could not possibly understand or interpret the spiritual significance of this truth. The so-called human mind can understand nothing of itself because it has no genuine existence. Only the mind that is God can understand and interpret the Truth that is God. It does take the mind that is God to understand and respond to the Truths that are God.

Now we will go right into the wonderful *Gospel According to Thomas.*

Boundless Light and Love,
Marie S. Watts

LOVE

E'en though illusion may present
A picture of the world that's rent
And torn by anger, hate, and strife,
The Love I AM is all the Life
That lives, and all that can
Exist as that which we call man.
Illusion fades, and Light most dear
Reveals that Love is all that's here.

The Gospel According to Thomas

These are the secret words which the living Jesus spoke and Didymos Judas Thomas wrote:

1. And he said, "Whoever finds the explanation of these words will not taste death."

He who perceives the spiritual significance underlying these words of Jesus will understand that there is no death, that there is no birth, that there is no change. He who understands the spiritual significance of these words will know that there is no body that can be born, that can change, that can die. He who understands the spiritual significance of these words will know that God, eternal Life, is alive and is living as Its own individual Life; and thus, eternal Life, the Life that is alive as this Life, cannot die.

2. Jesus said, "Let him who seeks not cease from seeking until he finds, and when he finds, he will be troubled, and when he has been troubled, he will marvel and he will reign over the All."

To many of us, the search has seemed to be long, sometimes discouraging, sometimes filled with obstacles. Yet we have continued right on with this search. Why? Because we have no choice. We could not do otherwise. When this search has brought us to the standpoint of the Ultimate, we realize it has not been a search at all. Rather it is God who has been our entire life, mind, and consciousness being, who has been insisting upon revealing Itself to Itself as Itself. We realize this Self is the only Self in existence as our Self.

It reminds me of the search for the Holy Grail. All of us remember that story—how the searcher searched and searched; then he finally discovered the Holy Grail right back at the place from which he started. So it is with us. When we reach the standpoint of the Ultimate, we realize that every truth we seemed to be seeking has always been included in and as our own Consciousness. And instead of a search, it has been God, our own Consciousness, insisting upon revealing Its allness, Its completeness, Its entirety, as us.

Now, when Jesus said, "And when he finds, he will be troubled," what he really means here is that when we begin to discover that we really are every truth that we have seemed to be seeking, our seeming problems do not cease at this point; rather sometimes it would appear that the problems increase or seem for a little while to be more severe. But we who have learned to stand and stand and stand, despite all the seeming troublesome appearances, do come to the point of marveling. We so often say, "How wonderful this is. Can this really be true?" We certainly do marvel; but the greatest marvel of all is that it has been so simple, that it has been our very own being, and that we have not realized it before. And we do reign over all. We do know that what we know is power. In fact, we know that what we know is the only Power there is or can ever be. This is because it is omnipotent Mind, omnipotent Intelligence acting without opposition, without obstruction. It is in this wonderful consciousness of being that we can say, "My kingdom is not of this world." Thus we can realize that we are not under any of the so-called laws and cruel beliefs of a world of matter, of an experience of human relationships. Rather we know that our kingdom is our consciousness, and our consciousness is our universe.

3. Jesus said, "If those who lead you say to you, 'See, the kingdom is in heaven,' then the birds of the heaven will precede you. If they say to you, 'It is in the sea,' then the fish will precede you. But the kingdom is within you and it is without you. If you know yourselves, then you will be known, and you will know that you are the sons of the living Father. But if you do not know yourselves, then you are in poverty and you are poverty."

This quotation of Jesus is given in two sections. We will take up the first one first. "If those who lead you say to you, 'See, the kingdom is in heaven ... .' Here Jesus is simply saying that if we believe that God is in heaven and not where we are, then the birds are closer to God than we are. But Jesus does not stop there. He says, "If you say it is in the sea, then the fish will precede you." Here again, Jesus is trying to reveal that if God seems either above or below us but not our own being, the fishes themselves are closer to God than we are.

Then Jesus completes this when he says, "But the kingdom is within you and it is without you." Jesus is referring to the kingdom of God that is within the body because it is the body. He is also referring to the kingdom which is without the body because this kingdom is the All—it is the universe itself. Jesus is not deceived into thinking or believing that the kingdom of God is no more without the body than it is within the body. He realizes clearly that the kingdom of God is the heaven and the earth and the body itself.

Where he says, "If you will know yourselves, then you will be known, and you will know you are the sons of the living Father," he really means that in all your seeming search, it has been the God-identity insisting upon revealing Itself as our Self. If we know this Identity as It is, we will know ourselves to be the Life that is the Father, the Life that is the Son.

This Life is exactly the same Life—not two but one—which is the One alone. If you know yourself, you know you are the very same Life that is God. If you do not know yourself, then you do not know God, and you can certainly seem to be in poverty. Just to the extent that we do not appear to know God, to that extent we cannot be fully and completely aware of ourselves. That is indeed the only lack there could be. Poverty can only be a seeming failure to know that God is our only Self, that God is the only existence right now as the Self of you—right here as the Self of you, of me, and of all.

Actually, if we do not know ourselves, we do not know anything. If we do not know ourselves, we could not even exist because the only existence there is, is God Itself identified as our own Self-consciousness. If we do not know ourselves, if we do not know that God is all there is of us, that God is all there is of the universe, we not only are in poverty but we are poverty itself. Poverty would be non-existence, complete lack, complete absence of mind, of consciousness, of God. But we do know ourselves. Thank God we are increasingly knowing ourselves.

4. Jesus said, "The man old in days will not

hesitate to ask a little child of seven days about the place of life, and he will live. For many who are first shall become last, and they shall become a single one."

You know, that which is called birth seems to be the beginning of a dream or illusion that we live in a body of matter, in a world of matter governed by material laws. Now, we will not stress the dream, knowing it is nothing but illusion. Nothing that appears in or as the dream is genuine, has any reality, has any actuality. Nonetheless, it is necessary to say this.

The ones we call children find it much easier, much simpler, to perceive and understand the truth than do those of us who seem to have been in the dream for many years. Why is this? It is because they remember more. They remember more of what they were before the so-called dream, the illusion, began.

When anyone, to all appearances, is old and enlightened, he understands this truth, and he knows enough to know the child of seven days knows more than he does. As a matter of fact, he would only ask the child in order to be reminded himself just what he is of the eternal, changeless aspect of God which is his very being. Indeed, he is endeavoring to remind himself that there is no one old, no one young, no one in between, and that there is no beginning, no change, no ending for his specific Identity, or God identified as his being.

5. Jesus said, "Know what is in thy sight, and what is hidden from thee will be revealed to thee. For there is nothing hidden which will not be manifest."

How true this is. When we are able to see that which stands before us in the purity, the perfection, the beauty that it is, then that which seems to have been hidden will be revealed. When right where there seems to be density we see light, and light only, then that which seems to be hidden is revealed. When right where there seems to be imperfection, a blemish, a fault, sin, sickness, or even death—and yes, we can say birth, too—when we can see that which is right before us as all these fallacies and see the beauty, the changeless perfection that is God, then there is no hidden beauty; there is no hidden God. There is only God evidenced, God manifested, and we know it.

6. His disciples asked him, "Wouldst thou that we fast, and how should we pray, and should we give alms, and what diet should we observe?"

Now, you will notice here the disciples are asking about human means as an aid to attaining spirituality, but Jesus will have none of this. He turns them completely away from it in the following quotation:

Jesus said, "Do not lie, and do not do what you hate, for all things are manifest before heaven. For there is nothing hidden that shall not be revealed, and there is nothing covered that shall remain without being uncovered."

When Jesus says, "Do not lie," he knows the only lie that could be must be a lie to ourselves. What he is really saying is, "Do not deceive yourselves. Abide in and as the truth that is your only Self rather than the deception which appears to be yourself."

When he says, "Do not what you hate," he knows that in the consciousness of each and every one of us there is an awareness of that which is right, good, loving, honest, just, and principled. In fact, he knows the Consciousness of any one of us is God, who is all these things. What he means is, do not attempt to go against your feeling of that which is right. Do not attempt to go against God.

Everything you identify yourself with seems to be, or seems to become, your experience. Identify yourself as Love, and you experience Love because you are Love. Identify yourself as Principle, and your experience is a principled experience because God is Principle, and you are what God is. Identify yourself with eternality, and you realize you are eternal. Identify yourself as perfect Life, and the Life that is alive as your Life right here and now is perceived to be perfection itself. This is what is manifested. This is what is evidenced. And this right here and now is the kingdom of heaven. The kingdom of heaven is in you. You are in the kingdom of heaven because the kingdom of heaven is your consciousness.

I like the word *consciousness* for *kingdom*. The consciousness of your genuine, eternal, perfect, and only Identity is heaven itself. Indeed, there is nothing hidden that shall not be revealed. There is nothing that is covered that shall remain covered. The Truth, the very fact of the presence of perfection—eternal, changeless—is right here and right now, and that which appears to be matter cannot cover this Truth. This Truth is uncovered because the spiritual Consciousness that is this Truth is aware of Itself and is aware of being this Truth. Do you know, sometimes there seems to be a miracle here.

Let us call *mirage* that which seems to be a body of matter, material objects, and that which appears to be a world of matter. This mirage would appear to be something that could interpose itself between this glorious universe of Spirit, God, and our realization of it. In fact, it would tend to make us believe that which we are seeing is dense, heavy, dark, imperfect instead of light, beauty, and eternal perfection.

It would appear to us sometimes that that which we call a body of matter could superimpose itself into our consciousness, that it could cover the genuine and only body of Spirit, of Life. It would seem it could act as an obstruction to our seeing, to our perception of this body, this perfect, beautiful, glorious body of Light that is right here; but what Jesus is trying to tell us here is that there is no body of matter. There can be no material objects that can get in our way or conceal from us, hide from us, the true, genuine, and only universe world, being the only body in existence. Indeed, there is nothing hidden.

That which seems to be matter can hide no aspect of God; neither can it hide God, being all there is of us, including our bodies. And it is in this realization that what seems to have been covered over with matter or material appearance or deception—what actually exists—is uncovered. As we realize this truth, the perfect, eternal, glorious body of Light appears, is realized, is recognized, and is known to be the only body in existence; and this is just as true of the body of the stars and planets; just as true of the bodies of the animals, the fishes; just as true of the body of anything that appears in form.

I like the word *design* or *delineate* better than *form* because it gives a better concept of the way these bodies really are when we see them as light, as consciousness, as beauty, as the glory that is God Itself.

7. Jesus said, "Blessed is the lion which the man eats, and the lion will become man; and cursed is the man whom the lion eats, and the lion will become man."

The lion is always referred to as strength, as power, as perfection, as the king of the kingdom, and so forth. As we partake of this, as we realize this truth, it becomes our entire being. It becomes our very flesh; it becomes our very body; it becomes our experience. Not that it actually becomes all of these; it is that it has always been all of these, and we discover it to be our entire being. In fact, the truth itself is that which is called man, and we discover we are this power. We are the king. We are the strength. We are the Omnipotence Itself just as long as there is no little self, no pseudo-identity, no mistaken identity trying to be something of itself.

But where Jesus said, "Cursed is the man whom the lion eats, and the lion will become man," what he really means is that once we have realized the power of this truth, we cannot use this power selfishly. We cannot use this power to place ourselves upon a pedestal. We cannot use this power in an attempt to place ourselves above any other identity.

All of us know of those who have partaken of this truth, and then they have come to the point where they thought they could use this truth to gain anything. This is wrong. We cannot use this truth to gain anything. We are this truth. If we are not this truth, we are nothing. We do not use our lives; we are Life Itself. We cannot use this truth for any selfish purpose. Certain it is that we cannot use this truth in an effort to gain students or a following or to glorify ourselves.

8. And he said, "The man is like a wise fisherman who cast his net into the sea and drew it up from the sea full of small fish. Among them he found a large and good fish. He threw all the small fish down into the sea and chose the large fish without regret. Whoever has ears to hear, let him hear."

We might call this a case history of our own experience. All of us have gone through many of these so-called systems of metaphysics that are dual. We have accepted them, believed them, gone along with them; and every so often we would find some genuine truth that was our truth in them. We realize now that all these teachings have had their purpose in our experience and we are grateful for them; but we also realize that because they were incomplete we could not stop with any one of them.

When we come to this point, here we realize God really is All, All really is God, and there is nothing in this universe that is not God being that. Then we cast aside all the dualistic approaches called metaphysics or whatever, and we accept this one glorious truth. We have no regrets. We would not turn back if we could. Once we have seen the Light, the partial light does not interest us anymore at all.

In other words, we discard all dualism for the complete truth. We go all the way. The truth is here impartially for each and every one of us, and we are willing to go all the way. Otherwise we would not be at the standpoint of the Ultimate, which means Self-revelation, or revelation from within the individual consciousness itself. Jesus said, "Whoever has ears to hear, let him hear."

9. Jesus said, "Now, the sower went out; he filled his hand; he threw. Some seeds fell on the road; the birds came and gathered them up. Others fell on the rock and did not take root in the earth and did not produce ears. Others fell on the thorns; they choked the seed and the worms ate them. And others fell on the good earth and it brought forth good fruit. It bore sixty per measure and one hundred twenty per measure."

Whoever is prepared to hear, let him hear. We used to think it meant that it would not do any good to present to this one or that one because of lack of receptivity. This is what reveals itself here. There is no one who is not actually ready for this truth, but it does seem there are different degrees of awareness of this readiness.

We are not disturbed. It makes no difference at all if our truth, or the truth we reveal, does not seem to bear fruit. It makes no difference if it is not understood or if it does not seem to be understood; or if it does not seem to bear fruit or even if it's cast aside. This is all right because they will accept to some extent. They cannot help this. They will accept it, to the extent of their spiritual awareness, anyway. Having spoken, that is our only concern; having spoken, having shared it, we rest in our consciousness. This sharing of this truth is fulfilling its purpose.

We are not responsible for the fulfillment of this purpose. We are not concerned about it. We know when to speak; we know when to keep silent because we are the Intelligence that is God in action. We know what to say; we know what not to say. We are wise as serpents and harmless as doves, for we are Love Itself. We are intelligent Love, and we are loving Intelligence. And in our sharing of this truth, we find one here and one there who is fully open. He is ready to let his own consciousness of his God-being reveal itself completely. Then we find this one realizes his joy, his peace, his perfection; and not only that, he realizes them in abundance. There is great abundance of all that is good in and as his experience because he knows he is his own abundance.

10. Jesus said, "I have cast fire upon the world, and see, I guard it until it (the world) is afire."

What Jesus really means is, "I am the light of the world. In me there is no darkness at all," and this is true of us, too. We are the Light that lights the world in all its seeming difficulties and darkness. We are the Light that lights the world, and we guard It. We go right on being this Light no matter how difficult things may seem to be. We go right on guarding our Light, being alert, being the Light we are until the whole universe is completely Light. We are the Light of our universe.

What we are seeing right here is more powerful than all the summit meetings there can be; more powerful than all the political conventions there can be. The Light we are is the Light that lights the world until the world itself knows itself to be Love; knows itself to be at peace because it is peace; knows itself to be indestructible, imperishable Light. How true it is that the Light Jesus knew himself to be, that lighteth the world, is the Light that is still glowing, still shining, still active, enlightening the world—and there is nothing that can oppose it.

11. Jesus said, "This heaven shall pass away, and the one above it shall pass away. The dead are not alive, and the living shall not die. In the days when you consumed what is dead, you made it alive. When you come into the light, what will you do? On the day when you were one, you became two. But when you become two, what will you do?"

Yes, all that appears to be material or matter in form will be revealed as nothing; and the one above it—not matter but so-called human mind or mortal mind—it shall be revealed and is being revealed to be non-intelligence rather than intelligence, so it too is passing away. It is disappearing into the nothingness which it has always been. That which appears to be a material universe, stars, planets, all of this passes away when we see there is no matter.

Then there is the belief of material laws governing matter. There is also a belief in a mental hell and a mental heaven. This too passes away in our consciousness, that each one of us is his own heaven, and there is no hell. We need to know there is no more mental heaven than there is a material heaven. We see through all of that. We see that the only heaven there is, is our own consciousness, but we also see this consciousness is the consciousness of everyone, everything in existence.

Jesus refers to matter as "the dead." He says, "In the days that you seemed to drop into the dream, when the mirage appeared as matter, in those days when you made this acceptance of matter, you gave it all the life it had." Matter never had life of its own. The only life it appeared to have was the life you gave it with your acceptance of it. It is when you made nothing appear to be something—then you were the one, or seemed to be the one, in the dream who gave it life, but when we come into the Light, when the Light that is God is revealed to be our Consciousness, we know there is no matter to have life or to be made alive. Neither is there matter to be made dead.

Lastly, you were already that one Mind, that one Consciousness, even when you seemed to be born; but at birth it would appear that you became two, that you became dual, that you became life and body, soul and body. Then you accepted God and man. But when you seemed to become two, what did you do? The glorious, eternal God-identity that you had always been, that you remembered being, just insisted on revealing Itself to Itself as your being anyway. And this is what is going on right now. This is what we do even when we seem to be two.

27

12. The disciples said to Jesus, "We know thou wilt go away from us. Who is it who shall be great over us?" Jesus said to them, "Wherever you are, you are to go to James the righteous, for whose sake heaven and earth came into being."

Right here it is apparent that the disciples were thinking of Jesus as a person, as a personal master or leader, and feeling that Jesus must die or be apart from them. They were also asking who shall be their master or leader. It is apparent they were thinking of a person as a leader. They were thinking of a personal sense of the Christ, the Truth that was their own consciousness. Now, Jesus instantly recognized this and tried to turn them away from a personal sense of this Truth or of Its interpretation of Itself.

James is considered to be the highest spiritual consciousness. Jesus was trying to tell them, "No matter who you might seem to turn to, actually you are turning to the high, spiritual Consciousness, to the supreme One, the only supreme Consciousness, which is your own Consciousness." Certain it is Jesus was not speaking of James as a person, but he was trying in the only way possible to reveal to them that they were to turn to their own Consciousness of *being*—God Itself identified.

13. Jesus said to his disciples, "Compare me to someone and tell me whom I am like." Simon

Peter said to him, "Thou art like a righteous angel." Matthew said to him, "Thou art like a wise man of understanding." Thomas said to him, "Master, my mouth will not be capable of saying whom thou art like." Jesus said, "I am not thy master. Because thou hast drunk, thou hast become intoxicated from the bubbling spring which I have measured out." And he took him and withdrew, and he spoke three words to him.

Now when Thomas came to his companions, they asked him, "What did Jesus say to thee?" Thomas said to them, "If I tell you one of the words which he said to me, you will take up stones and throw at me; and fire will come from the stones and burn you up."

Here Matthew is seeing Jesus as an intelligent man with intellectual understanding of good, of God, but you remember that Thomas is the spiritual identity. How well Thomas knew that there was no way, there were no words with which to describe the spiritual Consciousness that was appearing right there as the one they were calling Jesus. Nevertheless, Jesus had perceived that Thomas had called him by the name of Master.

Thomas had drunk (had become drunk) from the bubbling spring which Jesus had measured, and this gives a wonderful conception of that which we have called teacher. "Thou hast already been, and will always be, the very same bubbling spring, or spiritual Consciousness, that I have been pouring forth to you, to your perception." And this is why he says, "I am not thy master."

Jesus well knew he was no different, no other than the disciples. He knew he was neither above them nor below them. He knew he was exactly the same Consciousness identified that was identified as each disciple and as each one who exists. Jesus knew all of this.

Actually, he never placed himself in the position of master. Jesus never looked up to anyone; neither did he look down at anyone. He knew better. He knew he was not master. He knew he was the same God-Consciousness identified that was identified as each disciple and as each one that could possibly ever exist. Jesus knew all of this. He knew each one is his own master because each one is his own God-being. The "bubbling spring" is also spiritual inspiration. Each one of us is our own renewal. Each one of us is our own purity.

And then Jesus took Thomas and he withdrew; he spoke three words to him. Now, when Thomas came to his companions, they asked him, "What did Jesus say to thee?" Thomas said to them, "If I tell you one of the words which he said to me, you will take up stones and throw at me; and fire will come from the stones and burn you up."

What were the three words Jesus spoke to Thomas? Those three words were the words we can only speak when it is God Itself speaking. They were, "I am God." And when God speaks these words, it cannot be any so-called human being speaking. Only God can say, "I am God." And when God says, "I am God," then and only then is when the mountains, no matter in which form they appear—even mountains which appear to be evil—are shown to be nothing.

It is only in complete illumination that we realize that of ourselves we are nothing, know nothing, can do nothing. Then we realize that because God is, we are, and only because God is Life can we be alive. Only because God is Mind can we be intelligent. Only because God is Life, Truth, and Love can we live, can we exist as fact. Then we can be loving. Only when we realize this, can we say in the quiet of our contemplation, "I am God."

Thomas knew better than to tell this to the other disciples. He knew they were seemingly too occupied with the personal sense of life to understand what he was saying. He also knew that if he told them, they would turn on him; they would try to destroy him. But he knew that the truth he saw was, and is, indestructible. He knew that the

31

God that was his being could not be destroyed. Rather the only destruction there is, is self-destruction, and he knew the very effort to destroy him would turn upon themselves and destroy them. So Thomas very wisely refrained from telling them the three words that Jesus had spoken to him.

Herein, dear ones, is a lesson for each and every one of us. The only destruction there can be is the illusion's destruction of the illusion; the mirage's destruction of the mirage; the dream's dissipation of the dream—but this never touches one of us. Actually, it never really goes on. It has no basis in fact. It is entirely fiction with no truth in it. That dualistic sense that claims to be a mortal or human man will always appear to turn on the one who says, "I am God." In the silence of our full illumination, we know that it is not I that speaketh but God that speaketh as us.

14. Jesus said to them, "If you fast, you will beget sin for yourselves; and if you pray, you will be condemned; and if you give alms, you will do evil to your spirits. And if you go into any land and wander in the regions, if they receive you, eat what they set before you, heal the sick among them. For what goes into your mouth will not defile you, but what comes out of your mouth, this is what will defile you."

Here again, Jesus is trying to turn them away from all the material sense of gaining or acquiring spiritual understanding. Here he says that if you fast, you must believe that by refusing matter as food, you will become more spiritual. Jesus knew that any so-called materialistic means of acquiring spiritual consciousness was wrong because it seemed to separate the one from the Consciousness he already was and had.

And when Jesus said, "When you give alms you will do evil," he knew that in the very giving of alms, they were limiting the one to whom they gave. They were saying, "I have something this one does not have, so if I give alms, it will give me a place in heaven, and isn't it too bad they don't have as much as I do?" But Jesus tells them to go into any land and wander in the regions; just to go about their daily affairs normally. Let their light shine, be what they are. Don't try to make your light shine. Jesus says in substance, "Be yourselves. Go about your lives in a perfectly normal way, knowing it is God that lives in you, through you, and as you; and don't attempt to be more of yourself by praying to a God outside yourself or by fasting or by giving alms."

Jesus said, "For what goes into your mouth will not defile you, but what comes out of your mouth, that is what will defile you." He is saying here that you cannot take anything from outside your own consciousness, for your consciousness is your universe; but he is also saying that if there appears to be evil within your consciousness, it will seem to appear not only as your body, as your mind, but it will seem to appear as your entire experience, as your universe. This, he says, is what will defile you. Whatever you seem to entertain as consciousness will seem to defile you—but, thank God, it never touches the God-identity that you are.

15. Jesus said, "When you see Him that was not born of woman, prostrate yourselves upon your face and adore Him. He is your Father."

Yes, when we can look at the one who stands right before us and see this one as he is, as God Itself, as Mind, as Life, as Consciousness, as Soul, we will be seeing Light appearing in form. When we see this standing before us rather than man with "breath in his nostrils," who seems to be born of woman, then we can see God right before us, and we can adore this one because we adore God. Not that we adore a God outside our being. If we adore God, we adore ourselves. If we adore God, we adore everything and everyone.

16. Jesus said, "Men possibly think that I have come to cast peace upon the world, and they do not know that I have come to cast divisions upon the earth: fire, sword, war. For there shall be five

in a house: three shall be against two and two against three, the father against the son and the son against the father, and they will stand as solitaries."

Jesus knew there was no peace in duality. He knew there could be no peace so long as there was the belief, the dream, the illusion, that there was God *and* man. He knew there could be no peace so long as we seemed to be deluded that there was a material universe, a material world, and a spiritual universe, a spiritual world. He knew there could be nothing but war so long as there was a belief that there was a divine *and* a human mind. He knew that wars were inevitable in this kind of illusion, and he was trying to reveal the fallacy of any hope for peace until this truth is seen — that there is one universe, one world, one being, and this is God-being. Jesus realized that always in duality there is the claim of division, of separateness.

Jesus knew that that which we call the five senses is that which gives the reports of duality to us. He also knew that it is because of these five senses that there seems to be separation and division in our existence. He knew so long as there seemed to be human birth there would also appear to be human relationships, and he knew that in these relationships there must be divisions; there must be inharmonies, so long as they were considered to be separate minds, separate consciousnesses, separate religions and separate lives. He knew that this, carried further, meant separate ideologies.

He was trying to tell them that instead of five physical senses, instead of man with breath in his nostrils, instead of separation, there is one sense, which is Soul-sense. There is one Consciousness. There are innumerable functions of this one Consciousness, but there is one sense, and this is Soul-sense. This is spiritual Consciousness, and there is no other consciousness.

In this Consciousness, there is no separation; there is no division. No matter how many identities there are—and they certainly are infinite—it is still one Consciousness, inseparable Consciousness, as each and every identity. Therefore, there can be no human relationships, no relationships of nations, no relationships of planets, stars, and so forth. Jesus knew that if they realized this, they would be aware of the fact that they were this very One. Here he goes on with this very same revelation, when he says:

17. Jesus said, "I will give you what eye has not seen and what ear has not heard and what hand has not touched and what has not arisen in the heart of man."

Here Jesus is saying, "I will help you to reveal from within your own consciousness the fact that the so-called five physical senses can only reveal a mirage without substance, without life, without activity, without form. I will also help you know there is no mortal or human mind, being, or body who knows anything or can do anything or can be anything."

18. The disciples said to Jesus, "Tell us how our end will be." Jesus said, "Have you then discovered the beginning, so that you inquire about the end? For where the beginning is, there shall be the end. Blessed is he who shall stand at the beginning, and he shall know the end and he shall not taste death."

How well Jesus knew that they were still believing they were born—that they were alive as a life that was born into a body of matter and they would have to die out of matter or have an ending. He knew that if they did not believe this, they would not be inquiring about it. That is why he immediately turned them to the realization that there is no beginning, when he said, "Where the beginning is, there is the ending." He is saying, "If there is beginning for you, there will have to be an ending. If you were born, you must die. If you know no beginning, how can you know an ending?"

Then Jesus is saying, "Blessed are we, blessed are you, blessed is everyone who, right in the midst of what seems to be a human life—a mortal man with all his difficulties and sorrows, sicknesses, births, and deaths—perceives we are eternal, changeless God, identified right here and right now, right even in the midst of the dream. Then we shall know there can be no death because there is no birth. When we see this right here instead of having to seem to pass through the experience called death in order to perceive it, we realize that we never even have to pass through what appears to be the experience called death; and it's about time we woke up to this fact. It has been right here all the while.

19. Jesus said, "Blessed is he who was before he came into being. If you become my disciples and hear my words, these stones will minister to you. For you have five trees in Paradise, which are unmoved in summer or in winter, and their leaves do not fall. Whoever knows them will not taste death."

Yes, blessed are we who know what we were before the so-called mirage, before the illusion called birth began. No wonder Jesus loved little children; he knew children remember more of what they were before the dream seemed to begin; and they really do realize more that they are this

God, identified right here and right now, than those of us who have seemed to go further into the illusion.

How well Jesus knew that if they really understood what he was saying to them, they would realize everything they see is their own consciousness, that there is nothing outside their God-being. They would see that no life is given to them and no life is taken from them. They would see that nothing is ever given and nothing is ever taken.

Furthermore, if we really see what this is, if we know this truth and know ourselves to be this truth, we are aware that even that which appears to be the stones in our existence, the stones in our substance, that which seems to be the activity of the stars, the planets, the earth, the activity of everything, is our own activity. Our own life, even that which appears to be the most dense, dark, hard substance, is recognized to be the same Consciousness, the same Spirit, the same Life that is our substance. There is nothing withheld from us.

This is a wonderful lesson for those who feel they lack something, particularly for those who feel they lack the necessary supply to carry on normally. When we really realize that our consciousness is our universe, our consciousness is everything we see, we then know we cannot be separate from, be separated from, anything that is essential to our completeness. We know our consciousness is complete because God is complete. Thus, all the supply that we could possibly need or use is already present, and known to be present, in and as our very own consciousness.

The five trees which Jesus spoke of are symbolizing the five physical senses. He is again telling us that instead of these senses reporting to us all sorts of pictures, false as they are, there is one sense which is spiritual sense, God-Consciousness Itself.

Now, he is telling us that when we are enlightened (or in illumination) we see things as they actually are rather than as they appear when we seem to be seeing through that sense which is called human vision. This ability to see things as they actually are is a spiritual function. It is this one Consciousness, the spiritual Consciousness, the only Consciousness, functioning as that aspect of Itself which we misinterpret as vision.

Jesus was aware of this. He knew this is a spiritual faculty, and it is present in and as each of us. It was this that enabled Jesus to see—right where the withered hand appeared to be, to *see* the perfect hand that needed no healing. It didn't need to change in order to be the perfection that it already was. Spiritual consciousness functioning as vision or perception is that innate faculty which enables us to see perfection rather than the apparent imperfection before us.

That which is called matter does not and cannot interpose itself in this Consciousness between us and that which we see. In the realization of that which we see as our own being, actually our own Consciousness, there is nothing called matter to come in and separate us from the clear, right perception of that which we see.

So often, illumination is referred to as though it were some great mysterious experience and something that could only be realized by very few. Nothing could be further from the truth. The only Consciousness there is, actually, is enlightened Consciousness. Illumination, enlightenment, is the Consciousness of each and every one of us. This is a spiritual faculty. This is the Christ-Consciousness, and It is just as much your Consciousness as it is mine or anyone else's. If we believe the fallacy that someone else has this Consciousness and we do not have It ourselves, we are right then limiting ourselves, or rather, denying our own spiritual Consciousness. Instead of that, let us claim this Consciousness because it is our Self. Let us claim our own spiritual faculty of being able to right here and now see things as they are rather than how they appear to be.

Any one of us who has ever experienced illumination or, more simply put, enlightened Consciousness, knows very well that in this Consciousness we never see anything that fades, anything that is in the process of destruction. We never even see anything that is in the process of beginning, of changing, or of ending.

It is an interesting fact that in illumination no one ever sees a baby, a child, or anyone old. All we see is constantly at its peak of perfection. We never see a withered leaf. We never see a withered blade of grass. We never see anything at all that can be interpreted as being imperfect. This, my dear ones, is the Christ-Consciousness. This is your Consciousness. This is my Consciousness. This is the Consciousness that enabled Jesus to see the perfect hand, regardless of how many stood around and believed there was such a thing as a withered hand. This is the Consciousness that stood beside the bed and knew the maid had not died and knew the body was Life Itself and could not die. This is the Consciousness that said to the maid, "Arise!" And it would seem to be true.

In this Consciousness, there are no seasons. There is no coming; there is no going; and particularly, there is nothing in the process of changing. Anyone who is aware of having, and even being, this illumined Consciousness cannot possibly believe there is such a thing as death because this one knows there is no such thing as birth. In this illumination we see, we know, we perceive the eternal, imperishable nature of all substance. Here we know there is no substance that is the kind of substance that can fade, change, wither, or die.

20. The disciples said to Jesus, "Tell us what the kingdom of heaven is like." He said to them, "It is like a mustard seed, smaller than all seeds. But when it falls on the tilled earth, it produces a large branch and becomes shelter for birds of heaven."

Jesus is saying here that there is nothing so small, so infinitesimal, but that it is God, all that God is, being that. Jesus knows that in this realization there is the revelation that the infinitesimal is the infinite, and the infinite is the infinitesimal.

However, there is something that is not given pertaining to this last quotation concerning the mustard seed. The kingdom of heaven is the universe itself. The kingdom of heaven is the stars, the planets, the infinite beauty and stillness of the desert, the ocean, the earth. All there is, is heaven. But heaven also is the smallest grain of sand. There is not so much as a pinpoint in eternity or infinity that is not the kingdom of heaven.

Everything, even from what the world would call a cell—a body cell, or any other kind of a cell—to a planet in the sky, has its purpose in being. It is Love fulfilling Its purpose. It is Love providing Its own protection, Its own defense against all the pretensions of what claims to be a material world, a material body, or a human being.

21. Mary said to Jesus, "Whom are thy disciples like?" He said, "They are like little children who have settled themselves in a field which is not theirs. When the owners of the field come, they will say, 'Release to us our field.' They take off their clothes before them to release it and to give back their field to them. Therefore I say, if the lord of the house knows the thief is coming, he will stay awake before he comes and will not let him dig through to his house of his kingdom to carry away his goods.

You, then, must watch for the world, gird up your loins with great strength lest the brigands find a way to come to you, because they will find the advantage which you expect. Let there be among you a man of understanding; when the fruit ripened, he came quickly with his sickle in his hand and reaped it. Whoever has ears to hear, let him hear."

Isn't it true that each and every one of us has said these truths when we have not really made them our own? These are "the fields that are not theirs." How long we have said, "God is All, all is God," and still not been fully aware of what we have been saying. We've been claiming this truth as though we had been claiming it from outside our own being, but we have not come into the consciousness that it is our being. So it was with the disciples.

Then Jesus goes on to say, "When the owners of the field come, they will say, 'Release to us our field.' "

This is so true. When our genuine and only Identity, our spiritual Identity, asserts Itself, which It does and is doing, we then refuse to surrender our Identity to something which appears to have the power to rob us of our God-identity. No longer do we surrender the field which is our being, our Consciousness, to the so-called material sense of life.

Then Jesus tells us how all of this is accomplished. Here the expression "take off the clothes" means that we simply discard all the dualistic arguments, the affirmations and denials, all the dualism of God and man, Mind and idea, and go on and possess the land. It is already ours, you know. The children in the field own it themselves, just as we are Self-possessed; just as long as we know we are God Self-possessed.

Now, the owner of the field is the genuine Identity. We do not need to make these declarations of truth about ourselves once we discover we are the truth—the very truth we have been saying. This completely eliminates any fallacy that we have to add knowledge to ourselves in order to have and to be what we already are. This does away with leaders and followers, teachers and students. This is the revelation that each and every Identity is complete within Itself. It is God, complete as that specific Identity, needing nothing from anyone else or from any other source.

Next, Jesus is saying that once we are enlightened, we are free completely of dualism. We stay awake; we stay alert. And these subtle arguments or appearances of evil cannot enter our house, or kingdom (kingdom being our consciousness), to rob us of our God-Consciousness, our God-identity. Jesus is also warning us not to make anything of the dream, because you will notice he says, "They will find the advantage which you expect." Of course, if we believe that the dream actually exists or there is a dreamer, we are expecting certain things to appear in this dream. But if we are wide awake, if we know we have always been awake, that there has never been a dream and we have never been a dreamer, then we cannot possibly expect anything to appear in or as a dream.

Once we are completely enlightened, we know there is no dreamer; there is no dream; there is no illusion; there is no deluded one. There is no such mind; there is no such consciousness. We do not make anything of the dream. Once we have acknowledged that there has seemed to be or to have been a dream, we stop this thing of honoring it. Once we know a thing, we don't have to go on knowing it and knowing it all over again—we *know* it. It is our consciousness. That is all there is to it.

It is the same as knowing twice two is four. Any time it is essential that twice two, or four, be active in our experience, here it is; but we do not go around all the time insisting twice two is four. And now, for instance, if a mistake should appear and someone should tell us that twice two is seven—why, we just know better. We do not go around day after day saying, "Twice two is not seven," or, "This is not a dream," or, "This is a mistake." We just know twice two is four, and this is all there is to it.

So let us do this very same thing in regard to this thing we call a dream. Let's not honor it; let's not dwell with it; let's not continue to seemingly make it real by acknowledging that it can even appear to be. We know it is nothing. This is all there is to it. We have already "girded up our loins with great strength" because we already know what God is. Knowing what God is, we know what we are.

Now, Jesus said, "Let there be among you a man of understanding; when the fruit ripened, he came quickly with his sickle in his hand and reaped it. Whoever has ears to hear, let him hear."

The sickle represents our readiness. We are ready. We stand prepared to see through the fallacy of any claim, any appearance of inharmony, and to see the perfection that is right before us. It is right in the very place, you might say, where the inharmony seemed to be.

22. Jesus saw children being suckled. He said to his disciples, "These children who are being suckled are like those who enter the kingdom." They said to him, "Shall we then, as children, enter the kingdom?" Jesus said to them, "When you make the two one, and when you make the inner as the outer and the outer as the inner and the above as the below, and when you make the male and the female into a single one, so that the male will not be male and the female not be female, and when you make eyes in the place of an eye, a hand in the place of a hand, a foot in the place of a foot, an image in the place of an image, then shall you enter the kingdom."

What Jesus is conveying here is that these children remember what they were. They know more of what they are, and they are like those of us who are awake, who are aware of what we are, of what we have been, of what we will always be. This next revelation is perhaps one of the greatest, one of the most beautiful, one of the most complete of any that has been revealed here in this *Gospel According to Thomas.*

What does it mean to enter the kingdom? It means to be completely conscious. It means to be aware as that spiritual Consciousness, that spiritual faculty of perception that knows Itself and the all to be just what God is and nothing else.

"When you make the two one"—in other words, when you can look right at what the world calls a body of matter and see a gloriously perfect, changeless body of light, of Spirit, a glorious body—then you have entered the kingdom.

"When you make the inner as the outer and the outer as the inner and the above as the below"—all right, here it is. When you know the substance of the body is God, conscious Life, Mind, Intelligence in form, and when you know the substance that is this body is not confined or restricted to the body—that it is the above and the below, the outer as well as the inner, that it is the universe itself—then you have already entered the kingdom.

Now, you might be questioning, "How is it possible for the outer and the inner to be the same? How is it possible for the substance, the essence, of the body to be the very same substance (essence) that is heaven itself?"

Let us remember one of the Bible verses in which God says, "Do not I fill heaven and earth? saith the Lord." And also there is David, the Psalmist,

49

singing, "Whither shall I go from thy Spirit, whither shall I flee from thy right hand? If I ascend up into heaven, thou art there." We all know God does fill the heaven and the earth. The substance, the essence, is exactly the same. The substance that is the heaven and earth is the substance that is the body.

In case this is not quite clear, let us take what we would call a human comparison. Any so-called human comparison is bound to be somewhat faulty because there is no matter which we can use for a comparison. But the following might help clarify the above.

For instance, right in this room there are several lamps and several light globes. The light which is within each globe is the light which is without each globe. Let us not consider what appears to be a material light element; but the light which is within the globe and the light which is without the globe is identically the same light.

And here's another point which might be helpful in this realization. It would be utterly and completely impossible to divide the light that emanates from one lamp from the light that emanates from another lamp in this room. One might compare the light which is within the globe to the light that is the body. Unless something draws our attention to the shape or the form of the globe itself, we are not even aware of the globe. Of course we know the globe is there, but we don't make a point of it.

The form of the globe is inconsequential, yet there is form. The light which is within the form is exactly the same light which is without the form. And thus it is that the inner and the outer, the above and the below, are the same—the same one. Each lamp, for example, is distinctly that lamp and none other. Each light which is within the lamp is distinctly that light. There is no material light. All light is immaterial. All light is spiritual, completely free of density.

It is in this way that we see the Consciousness which is the male to be exactly the same Consciousness which is the female. Surely, the male is distinctly the male function of Consciousness. The female is distinctly the female function of Consciousness. They each are aspects of the one Consciousness. Yes, when we see that the function of the male and the function of the female is not to create children or to bring about a continuation of human beings in or with bodies of matter, then we see these functions as revelations of the One. Then this is marriage, and it is beautiful. When we understand this, we are already in the kingdom of heaven—and we are conscious of always being in the kingdom of heaven, as well as *being* the kingdom of heaven.

It is this spiritual and enlightened Consciousness which enables us to look at what appears to be a material world, with what appear to be eyes of matter—but actually is the one spiritual eye—and see it as it is. When we see a spiritual hand where a material hand seems to be, this hand is the hand of Consciousness, Light, changeless perfection and beauty. And when we see a spiritual foot right where a material foot seems to be, when we see there is an image, a body, right where there seems to be a body of matter, there is this spiritual body, this body of Consciousness. Indeed, this is the body which is God in form right here and right now. We realize we are in the kingdom of God; the kingdom of God is in us because we are the kingdom of God.

We are our own universe. We are the power, the Consciousness that is always in control. This Consciousness reigns supreme within our own universe because we are Self-governed. The kingdom of God is our kingdom and we know it. We are the king of our kingdom.

23. Jesus said, "I shall choose you, one out of a thousand, and two out of ten thousand, and they shall stand as a single one."

This certainly sounds as though there was partiality, as though one could be chosen and another left out of the kingdom of God. Of course, this is impossible. Jesus did not choose us. Each one of us chooses to reveal himself as he is, and who is it who chooses to reveal himself or itself? It is God choosing to reveal Itself as Itself.

It is true there are not many of what you might call the world population who are seeing this truth all the way, as we are. We also could be called few in numbers, but this is of no importance. We have opened consciousness full to this point. Many of the metaphysical movements have much bigger crowds. There are many who have great followings, but there is infinite power in what we are seeing.

You know, the Bible says, "Where two or more are gathered together in my name, there am I in the midst of them." Even though we may seem few in number, "in my name"—recognizing that God is our Identity—the *I* that is the power, the *I* that is omnipotence Itself, is right here and omnipotently active as each and every one of us. It has Its purpose in being us, and It fulfills Its purpose through Its omnipotent activity, which is our omnipotent activity.

24. His disciples said, "Show us the place where thou art, for it is necessary for us to seek it." He said to them, "Whoever has ears, let him hear. Within a man of light there is light, and he lights the whole world. When he does not shine, there is darkness."

Here you can see that the disciples believed Jesus was in a different place, a different situation than they were. They believed he had something they had not and they must find it in order to have it; they must discover it from someplace outside themselves, someplace without themselves. This follows beautifully that which has been said just before this, in which the genuine meaning was that the Christ, I Am, appears as one here and one there, but still It is the only One. What Jesus is saying is that the Christ is everyone; the Christ is everywhere as each of us.

You notice Jesus said, "Whoever has ears to hear"—that is, whoever is prepared to hear, whoever hears with the inner ear, the spiritual consciousness—"let him hear."

Jesus said, "Within a man of light there is light, and he lights the whole world. When he does not shine, there is darkness." Isn't this beautifully impersonal? Jesus claims no Christ for himself that he does not claim for each and every one of us. He says the Christ-light does light the world. There is no darkness in this Light. The darkness is the delusion's delusion. Jesus says that as we shine, as this Christ-light shines as our light, it does reveal itself to be the Light of the world. It is the universe—our own consciousness, our own experience, our own body and its substance. The Light, the Consciousness, which exists as all

54

and also exists as this universe, are one and the same Light.

Do you know, this is the answer to what they call absent treatment. It is in this revelation—that the Christ is everywhere and everyone—that we perceive there is no absent treatment. There could be no absent treatment. It could not be. When instantly our attention is focused upon that one, any one, we realize him to be within our consciousness because he is our own consciousness. We are where that one is; that one is where we are, and there is no division, no separateness in our consciousness.

How then can it be called absent treatment? The Christ-Consciousness is not confined or restricted to or by anyone. It is the same Christ, the same Consciousness, and even though one calls upon an apparent other one for help, it is that he is actually calling upon his own Consciousness, his own Christ-Consciousness. If there were such a thing as absent treatment, it would be impossible to know the "treatment" reached anyone. It might reach and it might not.

This is the fallacy, the thing that is wrong about directing thoughts and the like. As long as we believe there is anyone other than the Christ--Consciousness that we are, we are going to accept the accompanying fallacy that this Consciousness can be clouded, that there is something wrong, that It is ill, that It is lonely, that It is in lack, that It is suffering, that It is fearful—all sorts of things. But once we know the very same Consciousness that is our Consciousness is even the Consciousness of the one who has called for help, we know there is no separation in Consciousness Itself and there is no absent treatment. There certainly isn't the possibility of a treatment being misdirected.

Incidentally, I do not like the word *treatment*. It is not a very good word. I like *conscious omnipotent perfection realized, revealed, manifested, and evidenced right here and right now.* This is all there is to treatment. In the foregoing quotation, Jesus says everyone is his own Light, and in us there is no darkness.

25. Jesus said, "Love thy brother as thy soul; guard him as the apple of thine eye."

Isn't this wonderful? Yes, love thy brother because thy brother is thy very Self. The Soul, the Consciousness, that is thy brother is the Consciousness that is thy Self. This is what Jesus is saying here. The opposite can be true, too. If it were possible for you to hate yourself, you would be hating your brother. If you hate your brother, you have to hate yourself. We should love ourselves just as we love our brother. Every time we seem to criticize ourselves, every time we seem to condemn ourselves, every time we say, "I am stupid," or, "I have no understanding," or, "I am dense," we are saying it about God, who is our Self. We are saying it about our brother, too, you see.

Claim your God-Self. Never criticize yourself. This is particularly true about remembering a past for which to condemn oneself. The very fact that you are condemning yourself would be the absence of the love that is already here. It is all right when you know it is God loving Himself. Indeed, we must love ourselves, even as we love our brother, but it has to be impersonal love.

Right now I am going to tell you something that has revealed itself recently. We must love the body. This does not mean, of course, that we must love a body of matter; there is no body of matter. But we do know how anything we love responds to that love. We know that when we love our flowers and our plants, they bloom; they smile; they are gloriously beautiful as we love them. When we love our animals, our fish, our birds, we know the response that is right here and right now.

Love cannot resist Love. Love responds to Itself, and we must love our bodies—not as a personal love but with the same kind of love with which we love our friends, our pets, our gardens; with which we love the beauty of a sunset. It is this kind of love with which we must love our bodies. We love all that God is.

Sometimes we hear someone say, "Oh, we have to get rid of this body." This is one of the most vicious misconceptions there could be because if we want to get rid of something, we certainly cannot love it. So often, when the body seems to be inharmonious in some way, there seems to be a tendency to resent it, even hate it; but dear, dear friends, neither hate nor resentment ever, ever revealed the perfect body of Light, of perfection, of glory which is your body right here and now; which is my body right here and right now.

Love reveals Itself as loveliness. Love reveals Itself as perfection, as beauty, as what It is—as God. So love the body as impersonally as you love God, your plants, etc., anything that you see. Love everything that you see. Love everything which is within your consciousness (your universe), which is your body.

26. Jesus said, "The mote that is in thy brother's eye thou seest, but the beam that is in thine eye, thou seest not. When thou castest the beam out of thine eye, then thou wilt see clearly to cast the mote out of thy brother's eye."

The interpretation of this quotation is a long, long way from the old orthodox interpretation from the Bible. If we seem to see something wrong with our brother, that something wrong is within our own consciousness. Our consciousness is what we are, so that something wrong would have to be something wrong with us. Once we see there is no one with something wrong with him, we are seeing clearly, and we are seeing that there is no imperfection within either our brother or ourselves. In this we are seeing that God alone is. God alone is identified, and in God as God there is no imperfection. There is no mote in the brother's eye, no beam in our eye. In fact, there is nothing to be cast out.

27. Jesus said, "If you fast not from the world, you will not find the kingdom; if you keep not the sabbath as sabbath, you will not see the Father."

This is true. To fast is to do without. To fast is to refuse to take in. To fast is to abstain from partaking of the illusion—the delusion of birth, materiality, change, and death. Once we are enlightened, none of these subtle illusions can find a response in us, and we are our own immunity to any of their fallacious claims. In this we have already found the kingdom; we already have discovered we are this Consciousness.

What is the sabbath? The sabbath is a holy day. The day is the Light, and we must see that the darkness and the Light are both alike. The Light is all there is; there is no darkness. Unless we see and keep this holy day, this holy Light—consciously,

constantly, and without interruption—we are not
going to see that God is what we are, and we are
what God is. In other words, we will not see that
the Father is our own Self.

**28. Jesus said, "I took my stand in the midst of
the world, and in flesh I appeared to them. I
found them all drunk, and I did not find any of
them athirst. My soul was afflicted for the sons
of men because they are blind in their heart and
do not see that empty they have come into the
world and empty they seek to go out of the world
again. But now they are drunk. When they have
shaken off their wine, then will they repent."**

Yes, Jesus could even take on what appeared
to be a body of flesh, a body of matter. He could
even appear as another human being to those who
seemed to be dreaming. He did this because it was
necessary in order that he could help remind them
of what they already were.

Then he says, "I found them all drunk." To be
drunk means they were not themselves. No one is
himself when he is drunk.

Then he says, "I found none of them athirst."
He found that they were seemingly so deluded by
the things of this world that they were not open;
they were choosing not to know what they were.

Jesus follows with, "And my soul was afflicted
for the sons of men." Yes, don't we yearn some-

times to help those who believe they are the sons of men, those who believe themselves to have been born into a world of trouble, into a body of matter that can be sick, can pain, that can suffer, deteriorate, and die? Yes, we also seem to be afflicted and yearn to help them. They seemed to be blind in their heart, and Jesus knew the only blindness there is would have to be a seeming lack of consciousness of what we are.

Empty means seemingly devoid of spiritual awareness. It would seem that at birth they were unaware of what they are, and empty they must go out of the world. If we continue in what seems to be the illusion until the fallacy of death overtakes us, empty we seem to go out of the world. But we are not deluded; we are not drunk. We are ourselves; we are awake.

When we have shaken off the wine and we repent, we come to ourselves and know ourselves to be what we are. This is all there is to it. There is nothing more that has to be done. Actually, even this is not a doing. This is conscious being.

29. Jesus said, "If the flesh has come into existence because of the spirit, it is a marvel; but if the spirit has come into existence because of the body, it is a marvel of marvels. But I marvel at how this great wealth has made its home in this poverty."

Yes. If a body of matter could come into existence because of Spirit, it would certainly be most peculiar. But how much more peculiar would it be if Spirit, Mind, Life, Truth, Consciousness, God were dependent on the appearance of a body of matter in order to exist, in order to be what It is? This indeed would be most peculiar—the marvel of marvels.

Then he says, "I marvel how this great wealth has made its home in this poverty." What a beautiful, beautiful statement—how this great wealth, this infinite, conscious, perfect, eternal, uninterrupted beauty and glory that is God should seem to be confined, compressed, restricted, boxed off in what appears to be a body of matter. Isn't it a beautiful realization? The marvel of marvels is that with all the fullness, purity, glory, and perfection that we are, we should have seemed to dream a body of matter that was subject to disease, to sickness, to deterioration, death, and destruction. Right here where this body of matter seems to be is this glorious, free, perfect, eternal, birthless, deathless, changeless body.

30. Jesus said, "Where there are three gods, they are gods; where there are two or one, I am with him."

Here he is saying that whether there are many or few is not important. It makes no difference. It is the same Christ being each and every one of us, the same *I* identified as each and every one.

31. Jesus said, "No prophet is accepted in his village; no physician heals those who know him."

Why would not a prophet be accepted in his own village? Why would one not be able to have his perfection revealed to him by one he knows or thinks he knows so well? Well, because when we seem to be acquainted with someone, we are much more liable to think of them as a human being—a human born of matter, of human mothers, human fathers—and they are subject to all the weaknesses and the fallacies that we are. We are so busy looking at what seems to be a human that we fail to perceive the God-being that is standing right before us. This is what Jesus means.

32. Jesus said, "A city being built on a high mountain and fortified cannot fall, nor can it be hidden."

It is true that we are still being fortified. It is true that revelation after revelation is still taking place or still going on in and as our own consciousness. No one of us claims to be aware that we are all of this Truth right now. Aren't we fortifying ourselves? Aren't we realizing our own strength, our own power, the purity, the perfection that we are? Aren't we learning to love our

Self more? Aren't we learning to love the one we call brother more? Aren't we having a greater realization that God is the All of all, as All—this, no matter in what form it may seem to appear before us? No, we are learning all of this. We are realizing all this.

Aren't we learning to place a value upon ourselves? Is this egotistical? No, it is diametrically opposite from the value we may place on ourselves as a human being. We are loving our Self. We are glorifying God, the city that is on the hill. This is what Jesus means by fortification. This is our defense. This is our own immunity to all the delusions and illusions of what would appear to be a human or mortal being.

33. Jesus said, "What thou shalt hear in thine ear and in the other ear, that preach from your housetops; for no one lights a lamp and puts it under a bushel, nor does he put it in a hidden place. Rather he sets it on the lamp stand so that all who come in and go out may see its light."

Now, we know what this other ear is. It is the spiritual faculty of hearing, when we hear spiritually and we recognize we are hearing our own Self, our own Consciousness. It is then that we can speak with power, speak with authority, because we are not speaking as a human being. We are not speaking as a mortal. When we hear with a so-called mortal ear, we can hear almost anything, either good or bad. When we hear with the ear of Consciousness, we hear truly.

You will remember Jesus said in substance, "What I hear, I speak." And with all sincerity, this author tells you I speak only that which I hear. Constantly I listen, and it is only because God speaks that the words can be spoken. But before this can be, the words have to be heard with the inner ear. They must be heard as this spiritual Consciousness, which is God being aware of Itself, God aware of expressing Itself, God aware of revealing Itself, even *as* the words that are being spoken.

Then Jesus says, "For no one lights a lamp and puts it under a bushel, nor does he put it in a hidden place, but he sets it on the lamp stand so all who come in and go out may see its light."

You will notice here that Jesus does not say that the one who lights the lamp sets himself upon the lamp stand. He does not say the one who places the lamp sets himself upon a pedestal. Rather he so impersonally says that he places the light upon the lamp stand.

It is true we cannot hide what we see. We cannot hide what we are. You know, we do not have to say a thing is true, just because it is. We do not have to say we know a truth, just because it is. If we are seeing it, we are being it, and those whom we meet are going to know we are being this truth whether we say a word or not. They feel it. They sense it. How can they help it? Actually, they are seeing themselves. They are sensing their own being.

Wherever you go, whatever you do, you are this Light. If you are actually seeing It, you cannot help but be It. Others might see this Light as a human being, a nice personality, or anything else. It makes no difference, and ultimately they are going to have to recognize this Light for what It is because they are going to have to see that It is their own Light. It is the Light which is their Consciousness—but it does take the Light to see the Light. So you see, it is being the Light that is seeing the Light, and it is seeing the Light that is being the Light.

34. Jesus said. "If a blind man leads a blind man, both of them fall into a pit."

If anyone tries to lead anyone, they are way off the beam. No one can be led into this truth. Anyone who considers himself a leader, who leads those he believes to be blind, is surely deluding himself. Those who place themselves upon a pedestal, hoping that others will look up to them, are sure to topple. Pedestals have a way of becoming top-heavy, and great is the fall thereof.

No one can look down on anyone. In fact, one would have to be blind in order to believe that he could lead another.

Here is something else that is being revealed: can anyone who is dreaming, or seems to be dreaming, awaken another dreamer? Anyone who believes he is entrenched in this apparent world of matter cannot possibly awaken another who is steeped in this same belief. It is absolutely essential we walk around in this seeming dream fully awake so we can awaken another in the seeming dream. It makes no difference how much compassion we have for another who seems to be in great difficulty. It is impossible for us to realize we are this great Light enough to awaken others unless we know ourselves that this is a dream and we are awake.

Furthermore, we have to know that they, too, are awake. They are untouched by the dream, and there is no dream or dreamer. This does not mean that we are cruel. We do not say anything unloving. We do not tell them that it is their imagination or to snap out of it. We say the loving thing. We say the compassionate thing and do that which is loving; but just the same, we stand in the spiritual Consciousness which knows there is nothing wrong.

35. Jesus said, "It is not possible for one to enter

the house of the strong man and take it by force unless he bind his hands; then will he ransack his house."

It would not be possible for us to be under all the beliefs of a human life, all the troubles and difficulties of a man with breath in his nostrils, if we had not seemed to be bound by being born; by the belief, illusion, and dream of being born. We could not think death inevitable if we had not been duped into the belief of death. This very claim, the lie, the fallacy that says we were born, is that which seems to bind us.

Incidentally, this is the same illusion which would ransack our house and seem to rob us of our harmony—rob our bodies of their peace and their perfection, their permanency and their eternality. It is this claim that would empty us, make us a vacuum, make us ignorant and make us unconscious of what we really are. It is this same illusion that would make us nothing, and that is just what death would have to be if there were death. This would be nothing, or nonexistence.

36. Jesus said, "Take no thought from morning until evening and from evening until morning for what you shall put on."

What Jesus means is that we are not to try to avoid this so-called dream by thinking, by reasoning, by making affirmations or denials. He is telling us that all that is necessary is for us to be conscious of what we are; that we know what we are and be what we know. This we be (are) consciously, staunchly, without interruptions and without doubt.

37. His disciples said, "When wilt thou be revealed to us and when will we see thee?" Jesus said, "When you take off your clothing without being ashamed and take your clothes and put them under your feet as the little children and tread on them, then will you see the Son of the Living One and you shall not fear."

It is clear here that the disciples were expecting and hoping to see a personal Jesus, a human being with a body of matter, but Jesus knew they could never see him as he really was, and is, so long as they were attempting to perceive the Christ, God identified and expressed, as the one who was standing before them. When we see the Christ as the one standing before us, we will also be able to see the Christ of our own being, of our own bodies, of our own entire experience.

Then Jesus says, "When you take off your clothing without being ashamed and take your clothes and put them under your feet as the little children and tread on them, you shall behold the Son of the Living One and you shall not fear."

Jesus is not speaking in a literal sense or a human sense, as though they were to take the clothes from their bodies of matter. This great truth Jesus is revealing has much greater significance, much more spiritual significance than that.

It does appear we are clothed in or with a body of matter. Of course, we know this is not true anymore than the body we appear to have in the night dream is the body we really have. But it is as though, in the illusion's illusion, we clothe ourselves with a kind of body we do not have. It is as if we superimpose something we do not have; something that is dense, heavy, dark, and materialistic over the body of Light that is our eternal body.

This is why the disciples could not see Jesus. This is why they were able to see him, even though they were not seeing his body of Light. They were seeing what they themselves apparently saw him in.

When we take off this clothing, when we are fully enlightened (illumined), then we do see the Light—the Christ which is our own being and body. Thus we are able to see the Light, the Christ that is the body of the one they called Jesus. Not that this Light is confined to the body—it is the eternal body that knows no birth, no change, no age, and no death.

As our consciousness of what we really are becomes more enlightened, we do put down our clothes as little children and see that we do lose all sense of a personal identity. We really are above and beyond all duality, all misidentification.

38. Jesus said, "Many times you have desired to hear these words which I say to you, and you have no other from whom to hear them. There will be days when you seek me, and you will not find me."

Always we have known this. Always this Christ-Truth has been included within and as our very own consciousness. If it were not, we would not even be conscious. If you are intelligent enough to lift a finger, you are intelligence. If you are conscious at all, you are consciousness. There is no other that can tell it to you but yourself. Throughout all this long seeming search, it has been our own God-identity insisting upon revealing Itself to Itself as Itself—and this Self is you.

"There will be days when you … will not find me." Yes, this seems to be true. There are days, many of them, when all seems dark, and we almost wonder if we have ever seen the Light that we are. It does seem that the more Light we are conscious of perceiving, the more we are aware of that which seems to be darkness when it does appear. It is very much like being in a room that is brilliantly lighted and stepping through the doorway into what seems to be dark night. It is because the light is so brilliant that the darkness outside seems to be so dense.

We really can rejoice in the realization that the darkness only seems darker because we have seen the Light. We have seen the Light we have always been and will always be. It is well to remember also that when the darkness seems the greatest and is followed by the Light (we always know it *will* follow), the Light is always brighter. It is always more glorious and beautiful.

You might notice that when you go into a brilliantly lighted room from the darkness outside, the room always seems more brilliantly lighted. Actually, this is not "seeming" in the spiritual perception of this. It does seem that the darker the illusion is, the greater the illumination which follows this illusion. So we can be encouraged. We can take heart.

39. Jesus said, "The Pharisees and the scribes have received the keys of knowledge, and they have hidden them. They did not enter, and they did not let those enter who wished. You, however, be as wise as serpents and innocent as doves."

Of course, the Pharisees and the scribes had access to all the sacred writings. Jesus knew this.

He referred to this as the keys of knowledge. But because the Pharisees and the scribes did not perceive or understand the spiritual significance in back of these wonderful sacred writings, they could not possibly help the others who came to them for understanding.

Any one of us with an open consciousness already has the keys of knowledge, when we know what it is that we are looking for. It makes no difference whether a person goes to church. It may be for whatever reason. They may go for selfish reasons or perhaps to socialize. Actually, when one goes to church, it is because they yearn to see, know, and understand this very truth. This is an inner yearning, and it is a paradox that they are yearning for that which they already are. Of course, Jesus knew that the disciples were much more aware of this truth than were the Pharisees and scribes.

Next Jesus warns them a little bit by saying, "You know when to speak, what to say, how to say it." Love is gentle and compassionate. Love never hammers, never pounds anyone. Love is Intelligence Itself and does not speak when and where It should not. Love, Consciousness, Mind, Intelligence knows when to speak, what to say, and says it.

40. Jesus said, "A vine has been planted without

the Father and as it is not established, it will be pulled up by its roots and destroyed."

Of course, Jesus knew the only destruction there could be would be the illusion's destruction of itself. He also knew this whole appearance of birth, change, age, and death was illusion and nothing else. He knew, too, that God had nothing to do with this illusion. In fact, he knew that God knew nothing about this illusion, so naturally it could not possibly continue, could not possibly stand. Ultimately it must disperse and dispense with itself. This is the only destruction there can be because God is All, and God knows nothing of destruction.

41. Jesus said, "Whoever has in his hand, to him shall be given, and whoever does not have, from him shall be taken even the little which he has."

This passage used to bother this author terribly; it seemed so unfair. But the revelation of the spiritual significance of this truth is wonderful to perceive. What Jesus means is that whoever has even the slightest enlightenment, whoever has even the slightest spiritual consciousness, is going to become more aware of what God is—thus what he is. We know this to be true, even though it would seem that when we started, we had only the slightest inkling of the gloriousness which is this truth. Even though it has seemed slow at times, this truth and light has gradually expanded and expanded and is still expanding.

Having that one little spark of Light, having anything at all in your hand, more is going to be revealed, and more is being revealed. We know each and every one of us is this complete Light, and in order to be conscious, we have to be conscious as this complete Light. It does seem, however, that for only a split second in the eternity of our being, this false sense of our being does darken our consciousness.

We use the word *expanding* or the words *consciousness expanding*, although this gives a false connotation. What is actually taking place is that by *being* the Light that we are seeing, the illusion's illusion (that did not exist) is perceived to be the nothingness that it always was. Thus, it would appear to be an expansion when actually it is a greater and more glorious realization of the Light which we are. We have always been this Light, and of course, we will always be It.

Jesus gives us a warning yet again. He says if we do have some small sense of being this Light and yet the little personal sense of "I" still refuses to budge (insists upon trying to be something or to do something of itself), it seems that even the little light we have will become darkened; but it is wonderful to know it is for only a little moment in eternity that this seems to take place. In truth, it never takes place at all.

42. Jesus said, "Become passers-by."

You notice he did not say to go out and try to influence everyone to see this truth the way you do. He did not say to try to get everyone to see the universe which is Light, the body which is Light, just because you see it. He knew those disciples were going to go around in what seemed to be a world of matter, and some of them were going to experience walking around in and as a body of Light. These disciples were going to have exactly the same kind of experience that many of us have.

Many of us walk around in illumination. Many of us know the seeming solid wood floor beneath our feet is not solid; it is not dense. Many of us who walk along the sidewalk know there is no weight walking along. Yet we go about normally. We become passers-by. As someone said of Jesus, he walked around in the dream awake, and this is exactly the same as we do. No one knows the difference because we don't talk about it. We just experience it. Of course those we meet, especially if we speak with them, feel something. They know there is something that to them seems strange and wonderful, but they do not appear to know what it is—so we become passers-by.

43. His disciples said to him, "Who art thou that

**thou shouldest say these things to us?" Jesus said
to them, "From what I say to you, you do not
know who I am, but you have become as the
Jews, for they love the tree but hate its fruit, or
they love the fruit but hate the tree."**

If we seem to be buried in the attraction to and
the love for the material world, we certainly do
not like the pains and sorrows that go along with
it. Furthermore, we do not want anything to do
with the genuine and only world there is — the
world of Spirit. In fact, many of us know those who
do greatly avoid any contact with the spiritual truth.
We know many of our friends who wouldn't be
dragged to this truth with a logging chain.

The second half of this saying of Jesus means
that if we love that which really does exist, we
have no further use for the world of materiality.
Once we have seen through it, it has no more
appeal for us. We just cannot give up anything
until we see through it. Once we do see through it,
it isn't a matter of "giving up" the world of matter
but seeing that the world of itself is nothing. First
the so-called world of matter loses all appeal for
us. Then that which seems to be a world of matter
just disappears from our consciousness and
experience, even though we continue to seemingly
walk around in the dream awake.

44. Jesus said, "Whoever blasphemes against the

Father, it shall be forgiven him, and whoever blasphemes against the Son, it shall be forgiven him; but whoever blasphemes against the Holy Ghost, it shall not be forgiven him, either on earth or in heaven."

What Jesus means is that if one does not know God, if one does not really perceive what God is, this is understandable. It is not a matter of being forgiven; it is a matter of being understood. If this one, not knowing what God is, does not know what he is, that also can be understood. But if one has no perception or refuses to accept the fact that only because God is can he exist, this indeed is hard to understand.

What is the Holy Ghost? We hear so much of the Father, the Son, and the Holy Ghost. Truly the Father is the Father; the Son is the Son; the Father is the Son; the Son is the Father. But the Father (as) the Son—the Father being Itself or Himself as the Son—is the Holy Ghost. This is what we must all understand. This is what we all perceive, as spiritual enlightenment continues.

45. Jesus said, "They do not harvest grapes from the thorns, nor do they gather figs from the thistles, for they give no fruit. A good man brings forth good out of his treasure; an evil man brings forth evil things out of his evil treasure, which is in his heart, and speaks evil things. For out of the

abundance of the heart he brings forth evil things."

The good man—yes, even that which is called man—already has this treasure because he *is* this treasure. The spiritual identity which you are is already entirely good; your life and experience must be completely good because your consciousness is your universe. Here the word *heart* means consciousness, and that which is your consciousness is that which is experienced in and as your universe and body. This is your treasure.

If you seem to abide in darkness, if you continue to claim an identity apart from and other than the one God identified, this is then the illusion's illusion (or evil—one and the same) which will seem to be evident as evil experiences, troublesome conditions of the body, business, or home. Because your Consciousness, God, is your universe, so it is that the illusion's illusion erects and builds itself into forms of its own illusion. But you are not deluded. You are not the one suffering these deluded illusions or evil illusions.

46. Jesus said, "From Adam until John the Baptist, there is among those who are born of woman none higher than John the Baptist, so that his eyes will not be broken. But I have said whoever among you becomes a child shall know the kingdom, and he shall become higher than John."

Jesus understood that John was a good and Christian man. He also knew John to be one of great spiritual enlightenment. This is why he said, "his eyes will not be broken." What is meant here is that because John is greatly enlightened, he will not see double. Thusly he will see beyond duality. We know of those who write or speak the most glorious spiritual truths, and then in the next sentence or paragraph descend into duality again. We cannot be two; we cannot see or be both. There just are not two of us.

levels?

The one who sees this truth and knows himself to be this truth knows there are no others who are not this truth. Yes, Jesus knew John to be a good man, but he also knew John appeared to be born of woman. John *was* beginning to see beyond the fallacy of birth. Those of us who know we were never born are more clearly conscious than the best so-called Christian who writes a book, lectures, or preaches a sermon. Why? We know what we are. We remember more. We are more awake to what God is as our identity, our being, our life, our experience and our bodies.

All of us know of Jesus' love for little children. He knew that the little child has not forgotten so much of what it is. The child is not so steeped in the illusion and is aware of what it actually is more than the so-called adult, no matter if he is a good Christian man, no matter even if he is greatly enlightened. To become as a little child is actually to arrive at the Ultimate.

To arrive at the Ultimate is to reach that point where there is no struggle, no labor, no doubt, no fear, no mental striving to realize something or to be something. The child simply accepts. It accepts because it knows more of what it is than the so-called average adult. Thus it is with us, as enlightened consciousness reveals more and more of our genuine Identity.

47. Jesus said, "It is impossible for a man to mount two horses and to stretch two bows, and it is impossible for a servant to serve two masters. Otherwise he will honor the one and offend the other. No man drinks old wine and immediately desires to drink new wine. They do not put new wine into aged wineskins, lest they burst, and they do not put old wine into a new wineskin, lest it spoil it. They do not sew an old patch onto a new garment, because there would come a rent."

Jesus is simply saying we cannot be dual, and if we say God is All, we have to go all the way. We cannot say there is God *and* man. We cannot say there is mind *and* idea. We cannot say there is God and anything else at all because if we go all the way, whatever we see we know it is God being that. That little word *and* in the middle always has the connotation of twoness, otherness. This is why the expression "mind and idea," although it meant much to us before, simply disappears from our spiritual vocabulary as we arrive at this ultimate standpoint.

Here we say "Consciousness identified," and it is so easy to perceive Consciousness identified as God-being. We cannot go part of the way. We cannot even say, "This is all very beautiful, and I wish I could believe it; I wish I could live it." We cannot help living it. It lives Itself. It lives Itself as us because we are It Itself.

We are alive, aren't we? We cannot say we are alive unless we know our being alive is God being alive as our Life. We are conscious. We cannot say we have a consciousness of our own; we have to realize that the only way we can be conscious is because God is our Consciousness. In this going all the way, we cannot serve both. We cannot mix that which seems to be the illusion with what we know to be the genuine, the truth.

"No man drinks old wine and immediately desires to drink new wine."

Once we are spiritually enlightened, once we have realized, accepted, acknowledged, and experienced the fact that God really is All and there is nothing but God, we are not attracted to dualism anymore. No longer can we relish the things of the so-called material world. We realize we are our own inspiration—we are the Light.

We do not confine the inspiration, the Light we are, by restrictions of any kind. We know the body does not confine us. There is no blocking off of the inspiration, of the Light, of the Consciousness we are. The new inspiration, the Consciousness that we are, cannot confine and there is nothing to oppose. We accept only that which goes all the way.

Now we are really enlightened. We have partaken of the wine, of the Consciousness we really are. And so we can never again turn to the old dualistic so-called methods of gaining spiritual understanding. We know also that we cannot apply this to a body of matter; in fact, we cannot apply it at all. All we can do is *be* it.

48. Jesus said, "If two make peace with each other in this one house, they shall say to the mountain, 'Move from here,' and it will move."

Yes, right in the midst of what seems to be the deepest illusion, the deepest dream or sleep, we can awaken and become conscious of what we are. This enlightenment can and does move mountains of what seem to be illusions.

Here the word *house*, as it so often does, refers to the body. If, even though we appear to be living in a body of matter, we perceive this body to be

Spirit, Life, Consciousness, Love, eternality, and perfection, this awareness is power. It is omnipotent power because it takes omnipotent Mind to perceive this right in the midst of the illusion. Indeed, this is power. Indeed, this does move the "mountains of illusion."

A further spiritual interpretation of the phrase "if two make peace with each other in this one house" really means here that what is actually the body of Light will appear to the seeming world to be a healthier, better looking and younger body of matter. But the one who realizes that his is the body of Light (indeed, the Light Itself that the world is misinterpreting as the body of matter) is really shining through.

49. Jesus said, "Blessed are the solitary and the elect, for you shall find the kingdom. For you have come from it, and you shall return there again."

Indeed, this is true. Before what seems to be the dream began, before that which seemed to be birth ever took place, we were in the kingdom. Now we are in the kingdom, and we are increasingly aware that we are the kingdom. Here the word *kingdom* means Consciousness. We are the Consciousness Itself. We are the Consciousness we were before what seemed to be birth. We are right now the Consciousness that we eternally are, and being completely awake, we do not taste that which seems to be death.

Here the word _solitary_ means _the one_. Solitary means he who realizes there is one Identity that can be identified, one Being that can be. He realizes he can never return to the kingdom of God because he knows he never left it. He is conscious of the truth, aware of the fact that the kingdom of God is his own Consciousness.

50. Jesus said, "If they say to you, 'From where have you originated?' say to them, 'We have come from the Light, that place where the Light came into being of Itself. It established Itself and revealed Itself in Its own image.' If they say to you, 'Who are you?' say, 'We are Its children and we are the chosen of the living Father.' If they ask you, 'What is the evidence of your Father in you?' say to them, 'It is movement and rest.' "

Yes, we have come from the Light, but we really haven't come _from_ anything. We _are_ the Light. The Light is revealing Itself in, through, and as our entire being. Here the word _image_ means body. The Light is revealing Itself even as a body of light.

Incidentally, never resent anything about your body. Whether it seems unattractive or subject to weakness, it makes no difference. Whether it seems to pain or age, be destructive, ugly, or clumsy or in any other way distorted, it is not true. Don't hate your body. Don't hate anything about your body. Don't quarrel with your body; don't resist it; don't oppose it. If you do, you are quarreling with God. If you hate your body, you are hating God. If you are resenting your body, you are resenting God. If you oppose it, you are opposing God.

Know this body of Light to be Spirit; know It to be Consciousness; know that It is eternal Life—and *love* your body. Of course, you know this author is not asking you to love a body of matter. This would be an entirely perverted sense of love; but if you have a body, it has to be a body of God. It has to be God. It cannot be anything but God because there is nothing besides God for it to be.

You love God, don't you? Love your body. There is nothing in your body that can resist Love. There is nothing in this universe that can resist Love. Anything that seems to be out of order, painful, weak, troublesome, clumsy cannot resist Love. If you love your body, it loves you because the Love you are is your very body.

When you look into the face of a dearly loved friend, you know you love them; you know they love you. Love your body in exactly the same way as you love your friend. You will discover your body is the very same Love with which you are loving it. Thus if you love your body, it loves you.

We know the power of Love. All of us have seen the perfectly wonderful things that take place when we just stand in Love; when we just love because we know we are Love. When we love this body, it is the same Consciousness revealing Itself to be this perfect body. The body knows the Consciousness that loves the body *is* the body.

To fear any so-called bodily condition is to hate. Fear traced to the very depths of its nothingness is hate. This has been proven. Anyone can look into the eyes of the most so-called vicious animal, and if they are completely without fear, the animal will not attack them. We do seem to be subject to seeming attack by that which we seemingly hate. When there is no fear, there is no hate. When there is no fear and no hate, there is no resistance or resentment.

It is the same way with the body. The body is its own loving Self. Nothing about the body can attack or pester you or trouble you. You love this body because you know you are loving God. You know the very love with which you love is the God-essence and the all of your body.

Yes, if they ask, "What is the evidence (the sign) of your Father in you?" you can say, "It is because I act, I am active, I am Life. But because the Life I am is God Itself, it is restful, peaceful, effortless, uninterrupted, continuous, constant, perfect being." Orderly, perfect, beautiful, harmonious activity is

87

the sign that God not only is *in* you but the evidence God *is* you. There is the evidence of peace, of joy, of inspiration. This certainly is the evidence of Life, and we do not have to work to make Life be and to remain alive.

51. His disciples said to him, "When will the repose of the dead come about, and when will the new world come?" He said to them, "What you expect has come, but you know it not."

heaven

The disciples were laboring under that old orthodox illusion that if you were good, after death you would rest or repose. They also thought this world, this universe which is constantly new, constantly renewed (but without a time lapse in this renewal) would appear sometime in the future. It had been a prophecy, and they accepted it as a prophecy, even though no such thing as a prophecy exists. All that is said to be prophecy, all that is said to be good, right, and stated as a true fact is true right now.

Jesus is telling them the restful, peaceful, unlabored, perfectly harmonious life they expect after death is already here. He tells them this new world is no prophecy. The constant newness, the freshness, the wonder and perfection that is this world is already here; but the disciples seem to still be asleep. They do not realize they still seem

levels!

to be in the dream, and they have not as yet perceived this ever-present new world.

52. His disciples said to him, "Twenty-four prophets spoke in Israel, and they all spoke about thee." He said to them, "You have dismissed the Living One who is before you and have spoken about the dead."

The disciples are telling Jesus that the twenty-four prophets foretold of a human being who was to appear in a world of matter and who was to be king. But Jesus said, "You have dismissed the Living One." Jesus knew that which appears to be life within a body of matter is dead. He knew it was death itself. He knew the only death that exists is the belief that Life, God, can be born into a body of matter, and also the dualistic belief that this Life can suffer, get sick, age, and die out of a body of matter.

He is telling them they have failed to see the eternal Life identified, standing right before them. Instead they have misinterpreted it and considered it to be death itself (if there was matter to die). In substance, Jesus is saying, "You have rejected the Life that is God, eternal Life right here. *I* am this Life right before you. You are not seeing the Life that is God right here. Nobody needs to prophesy the Life that *I* am. *I* am not a prophecy—*I am*."

53. His disciples said to him, "Is circumcision profitable or not?" He said to them, "If it were profitable, their father would beget them circumcised from their mother. But the true circumcision in Spirit has become profitable in every way."

Again Jesus is trying to turn the disciples away from their dependencies upon orthodox beliefs, material bodies, or anything that is done to a non-existent material body. But when he speaks of the true circumcision, this does have genuine spiritual significance. Circumcision is supposed to mean purification, or spiritualization, but Jesus is trying to tell them that the true circumcision of Spirit is something entirely different from what they believe it to be. True spiritual circumcision is the purification of the Spirit, or Consciousness. It is spiritual awareness. It is purification from any taint of materiality, duality; of any blemish or any slightest flaw. True spiritual circumcision means going all the way in complete purification.

Jesus says circumcision becomes profitable in every way. Haven't all of us discovered that when the illusions of materiality and of duality are seen through, dispersed, and dispensed with, more of God—complete good—is realized and experienced in our daily lives? Indeed we have. Indeed, this circumcision of Spirit is profitable in every way.

54. Jesus said, "Blessed are the poor, for yours is the kingdom of heaven."

Most of those to whom Jesus talked were poor, and he saw this great humility in them. He saw the openness, the receptivity to the Light he was saying and being. He knew they were far more open and enlightened than were the Pharisees and the Sadducees and the so-called educated ones who had much more wealth in what is called this world's goods.

55. Jesus said, "Whoever does not hate his father and his mother will not be able to be a disciple to me, and whoever does not hate his brethren and his sisters and does not take up his cross in my way will not be worthy of me."

We know Jesus did not mean this the way it sounds. We know Jesus proved by everything he said and did that there was no hatred in him and he knew nothing of hatred, so he did not mean this in a literal sense. He *is* saying that he who doesn't recognize that he does not have a human father or human mother doesn't even exist. We cannot know who or what we are if we continue in the deluded sense that we were born of human parents. As long as we mistakenly believe we have human parents or life, we will continue on to the final delusion, which is death.

When Jesus said "in my way," he means it is necessary to discern this truth in the only way it can be discerned—in the Christ way. We have to realize there are no human fathers, mothers, brothers, or sisters because there are no human beings.

56. Jesus said, "Whoever has known the world has found a corpse, and whoever has found a corpse, of him the world is not worthy."

Any of us who has come to know what the world of appearances, of duality is, has discovered this world is indeed a corpse. It is dead. It is devoid of mind, intelligence, existence. When we discover this, the seeming world of appearances cannot understand it. This is because this world is neither intelligent nor does it have intelligence. It takes the Mind that is God to understand, to perceive this God-filled universe.

We know, once we have perceived the truth that the world of appearances is nothing, that those who seem still to be wandering around in the illusory world cannot see us. They seek us, but do not find us. They cannot know we exist. The only way they can know of our existence is to know us as the eternal, glorious being of Light which we are. The darkness of illusion cannot perceive this Light.

57. Jesus said, "The kingdom of the Father is

like a man who had good seed. His enemy came by night and sowed weeds among the good seed. The man did not permit them (the workers) to pull up the weeds. He said to them, 'No, lest perhaps you go to pull up the weed and pull up the wheat with it.' For on the day of harvest, the weeds will appear, and they will pull them and burn them."

Yes, let each one go on with the truth he can realize at the moment. There do seem to be a lot of weeds. Dualism is the so-called enemy. Dualism is perhaps the worst weed, but we never argue about it. We do not say, "This is all wrong." Let the weed grow. If you do say something, you are very apt to confuse them. They have to see it for themselves.

That which is the truth is all that is necessary for us to know. We just know it, and we don't argue about it. We do not talk about it because we do not have to. We do not criticize the other one. We recognize their particular approach may be dual; we know each one of these approaches is just a path along the way. It is a path to the realization that God is All, and there is nothing but God. We do not try to influence them or change their course. To do so would seem to help them build a resistance to absolute truth.

If they make a false statement, we don't correct them. We don't say, "This is all wrong. The way I see it is the way it is, and you *have* to see it this way." We just know that if we attempted to argue with or correct them, we would be guilty of bringing about the confusion that would seem to darken for a while what light they have. We just let it go. We know there is nothing in existence that can interfere with them ultimately realizing fully the true God-identity they are. After all, it's not up to us to make God reveal Itself.

The "harvest" is God's complete revelation of Itself. In this realization, no weeds need to be pulled up or burned. No false beliefs have to be corrected. All that happens is the revelation that there are no weeds. There is no darkness. There is no evil. There is nothing in need of correcting. There is no need for healing, for there is no darkness—just God.

58. Jesus said, "Blessed is the man who has suffered; he has found the Life."

We know this has not been a bed of roses for any of us. It does appear that we have suffered greatly in many ways. In spite of this, we are discovering the very fact that even that which seemed to be the worst suffering was only God's way of pointing out to us that "*I* am all there is of this." We who have seemed to suffer so greatly have found the way, and we find we are the way Itself.

59. Jesus said, "Look upon the Living One as long as you live, lest you die and seek to see Him and be unable to see."

Look upon the Life that is God. Keep your consciousness alert, alive, aware of the fact that the only Life in existence is God. Continue to be conscious of this one Life; maintain and sustain it within your consciousness. It is in this Consciousness that there is no death because there is no birth; but if you do not remain conscious of yourself as the eternal, one God-Life, you will appear to return to the illusion of a temporal, separate life. If you drop back into the illusion, you are really not seeing at all because the illusion never sees. Remain conscious of the one Life.

60. They saw a Samaritan carrying a lamb on his way to Judea. He said to his disciples, "Why does this man carry the lamb with him?" They said to him, "In order that he may kill it and eat it." He said to them, "As long as it is alive, he will not eat it, but only if he has killed it and it has become a corpse." They said, "Otherwise he will not be able to do it." He said to them, "You yourselves seek a place for yourselves in repose, lest you become a corpse and be eaten."

There is deep spiritual significance in this speech given by Jesus. The lamb means purity without flaw, without fault, without blemish. Even as the lamb is being carried to be killed, so do each of us seem to be subject to falling into the illusion (dream) of death. So long as the lamb remains alive, he will not eat it. So long as we remain conscious of what we are, there is no seeming danger of us losing our God-identity in misidentification. As long as we remain awake, know our Identity to be eternal Life, we are not subject to death. Only if we seem to be buried, unenlightened, oblivious to the beautiful Life we are, do we seem to be subject to the illusion; but the illusion doesn't actually exist. Only in this fallacy called a human life do we appear to be carried off to death. In the realization of the eternality of eternal Life, we know there is no death.

Jesus said, "You yourselves seek a place in repose." Repose really means eternal Life, spiritual Consciousness. The word *place* here means an established fact, established Consciousness. There is no need to talk about overcoming death because death cannot be overcome. Death can no more be overcome than can birth. No one can overcome nothingness, and both birth and death are nothing. But we do see through death. We see through it by realizing eternal Life is an established fact, and It is without beginning or ending. Once we realize that, we are never threatened; we realize we are in no danger. Our conscious Life is never in jeopardy of that so-called last enemy.

61. Jesus said, "Two will rest on a bed; the one will die, the one will live." Salome said, "Who art thou, man, and whose son? You have climbed onto my couch and eaten from my table as if you are someone." Jesus said to her, "I am he who is from the Same. To me was given from the things of my Father." Salome said, "I am thy disciple." Jesus said to her, "Therefore I say, if he is the Same, he will be filled with light, but if he is divided, he will be filled with darkness."

self – same

Here Salome was seeing what she interpreted to be just another human being. She probably thought him to be a good human being, but still a human being. She asked him who his father was and if he hadn't just eaten at her table just as other human beings do. But Jesus was not accepting this. He said, "I am he who is from the Same." He was trying to tell her he was the very same One who identified Itself as her identity or anyone else's. Jesus continues to tell her that when she realizes she is the "Same," she will be filled with light; but if she is still divided, if she still believes she is Soul *and* body, Spirit *and* matter, she will seem to be filled with darkness.

62. Jesus said, "I tell my mysteries to those who

97

are worthy of my mysteries. What thy right hand will do, let not thy left hand know what it does."

Again, here is another way of saying be not dual. Do not accept two. Do not attempt to mix Spirit and matter, Light and darkness, Consciousness and unconsciousness, Life and death. It will not work. Know that the *I* that I am knows absolutely nothing about imperfection. Eternal Mind cannot know a temporary mortal mind. Eternal Life cannot know a temporary life that has beginning and ending. God cannot know a temporal body. This body I am right here knows its own perfection, knows its own eternality.

63. Jesus said, "There was a rich man who had much money. He said, 'I will use my money so that I may sow and reap and plant and fill my storehouses with fruit, so that I lack nothing.' This was what he thought in his heart. And that night he died. Whoever has ears, let him hear."

In one part of this statement, Jesus is referring to the fallacious dependence on a material world for wealth, happiness, joy—for eternal life. But beyond this, there is a far greater spiritual significance to this statement. Here is this rich man who is going to do all these things, and he says he is going to do all of them so he will lack nothing. This is the illusion of depending upon a so-called material world; building from what seems to be a human mind, he can become complete. To lack nothing is to be complete. True completeness is only realized when we realize we are the completeness which is God identified, expressed, revealed, evidenced, and manifested as our completeness. It has nothing to do with materiality. Again Jesus is saying, "Do not depend on the illusion of materiality for anything—not for your health, not for your happiness or joy, not for your wealth or peace, not for your life, love, or completeness. This seeming dependency can lead only to the greater illusion called death."

Again Jesus says, "Whoever has ears, let him hear," and again he means those who really hear, hear with the one ear—the ear that is God Itself hearing. Those with the one ear hearing are understanding and perceiving the truth they are hearing.

64. Jesus said, "A man had guests, and when he had prepared the dinner, he sent his servant to invite his guests. He went to the first and said to him, "My master invites thee." He said, "I have some claims against some merchants; they will come to me in the evening; I will go and give them my orders. I pray to be excused from the dinner." He went to another and said to him, "My master has invited thee." He said to him, "I have bought a house and they request me for a day. I will have no time."

He came to another and said to him, "My master invites thee." He said to him, "My friend is to be married and I am to arrange a dinner; I shall not be able to come. I pray to be excused from the dinner." He went to another and said to him, "My master invites thee." He said to him, "I have bought a farm, I go to collect the rent. I shall not be able to come. I pray to be excused."

The servant returned and said to his master, "Those whom thou hast invited to the dinner have excused themselves." The master said to his servant, "Go out to the roads, bring those whom thou shalt find, so that they may dine. Trades-men and merchants shall not enter the places of my Father."

The first invitee was too busy. He had business interests; interests in the so-called world of materiality. He had to be excused from partaking of the feast of Spirit already prepared.

The second person invited apparently had stated his presence was needed elsewhere.

Next, the spiritual significance of the servant repeating, "My master invites thee," is the announcement of the only Presence—the Presence which is all the good, all the abundance, joy, peace, eternal Life, all that could possibly be right here and now. We are more than invited; we already are guests because our Consciousness is the presence of It Itself.

The following invitee states that he has a friend who is to be married, so he has a dinner to prepare and therefore won't be able to attend. In other words, he had social engagements which were far more important to him than to attend the feast of Spirit already prepared.

The last person had bought a farm, and he had to go collect the rent, so the servant returned and told his master that all those he had invited asked to be excused from attending.

The lesson of the above is that seldom are we able to bring anyone into the truth by invitation. Virtually everyone knows about the truth. If they are ready, receptive, and prepared, they accept it of their own accord. Generally, they are too busy to be bothered to come into this truth just because we present it to them. True, it is right; it is the loving thing to do to speak of the truth to someone who seems to be in need; but the all-knowing conscious Mind we are knows when to speak and when to keep silent.

The master then told his servant to go to the roads and bring those whom he finds so they may dine. He goes on to say, "Tradesmen and merchants shall not enter the place of my Father."

This is a further revelation of the same truth—that almost everyone is aware there is this truth, and they come; they come of their own accord.

Jesus says, "Tradesmen and merchants shall not enter the place of my Father." This should not at all be taken in the literal sense. Jesus knew there were businessmen; he knew that good business is God being busy. Good business is Principle Itself, intelligent Principle in action. This, therefore, is no diatribe against business or businessmen. However, those who seek truth for the purpose of using it, those who seek truth for their own selfish purposes, cannot receive or understand it.

Yes, all are invited; all have an equal invitation to awaken. When they awaken, it is because they have seen the complete fallacy of the so-called dream. All of us are ready to awaken when the dream becomes a nightmare. We do all awaken. We always awaken; of this we can be assured. And the closer the dream is to being nightmarish, the closer we are to awakening. We can take heart in this, also.

65. He said, "A good man had a vineyard. He gave it to husbandmen so that they could work it and that he would receive its fruit from them. He sent his servant so that the husbandmen would give him the fruit of the vineyard. They seized his servant and they beat him; a little longer and

they would have killed him.

The servant came and told it to his master. His master said, "Perhaps he did not know them." He sent another servant; the husbandmen beat him as well. Then the owner sent his son. He said, "Perhaps they will respect my son." Since those husbandmen knew he was the heir of the vineyard, they seized him and they killed him. Whoever has ears, let him hear."

Of course, this refers to those who refuse the truth, those who are antagonistic toward it. It is true that those who teach and write as though there is God (and) man—the servant being something apart from God—find very little antagonism; often they have large followings. But the more enlightened the so-called teacher or writer of the Absolute is the more antagonism he encounters. This is because it is impossible for a proud, egotistical little person; it is impossible for him to accept that of himself he can be nothing, and because only God is, can he be.

Something further to be considered is the realization that the Father and the Son are exactly the same One. This causes many to say we are sacrilegious or that we espouse the spirit of the antichrist. This is the same attitude which seemed to convict Jesus—Jesus knowing he and his Father were one. But Jesus knew God to be his entire

being and that he was just what God is and nothing else.

Of course, this seemed to arouse all the antagonism of the multitudes, but the wonderful thing to realize is this: in the first place, this antagonism is not intelligence, and it cannot direct itself. It has no desire to direct itself. It is not mind; therefore it is non-existent. Even its claim of being cannot be directed to the God I am, you are, because non-intelligence cannot direct itself against intelligence. It is just another way of saying the darkness cometh not to the light. Of course it can't. If the darkness were to come to the light, there would be no darkness. Do not be concerned about this because it *will* be revealed that there is no darkness at all.

66. Jesus said, "Show me the stone which the builders have rejected; it is the cornerstone."

Do you know what the stone is that the builders rejected? There is no birth. Of all the statements of truth, this is the one most adamantly rejected, but this *is* the cornerstone. It is because there is no birth that there is no life in matter. There is no life that enters matter, that can exist in matter, or die out of matter. The truth that there is no birth is the cornerstone, and it is this truth that enables us to know there is no death.

67. Jesus said, "Whoever knows the All but

fails to know himself lacks everything."

It makes no difference how much of the Bible we can recite from memory. It makes no difference how long we have been studying in the meta-physical field. It makes no difference how spiritual we think we are or how far along we think we are. Unless we know what we are, we don't know anything. To know nothing is to lack everything. To know what we are is to be what we are. When we know what we are, we know what God is. Transversely, when we know what God is, we know what we are. Thus we have all because we are all, and we know ourselves to be this All.

68. Jesus said, "Blessed are you when you are hated and persecuted; and no place will be found there where you have been persecuted."

There is only one place, and this place is where *I* am. Essentially he is saying, "In my presence there is no persecution. The established Consciousness that I am knows only this truth. If someone seems to do something to me that is unfair, then it is their problem—not mine. If I permit myself to be resentful of something that is unjust, then it is my problem. I cannot permit myself the luxury of resentment toward anyone or anything. Thus I have no problem."

The above is true of you. If you are claiming your own God-identity, you are claiming your immunity to every seeming problem. This immunizing of yourself includes your immunity to every seeming trouble, to every seeming criticism, to every seeming injustice. Why? Because you know what you are. In knowing your identity, you know that you are the Mind that is the power that knows Itself and knows Itself only. What is Itself? Itself is God-being.

69. Jesus said, "Blessed are those who have been persecuted in their heart; these are they who have known the Father in truth. Blessed are the hungry, for the belly of him who desires will be filled."

Blessed are we if we stand in solid conviction. We stand right in the face of any so-called evil appearance and refuse to accept it; refuse to hate it; refuse to honor or resist it. We do not believe it has existence. In this way we find God really is our identity, and we are indeed blessed. This is what it means to be persecuted in the heart. Actually, there is no persecution. We stand in the Light because we are the Light, refusing to accept any appearance of darkness. Yes, we are indeed blessed. We realize we truly are the Truth which is God being us.

"Blessed are the hungry ... ." Even that which we interpret as hunger for God, sometimes expressed as hunger of God, is God Itself insisting upon revealing Itself as ourselves. We are filled. We discover we are God-filled, fulfilled.

70. Jesus said, "If you bring forth that within yourselves, that which you have will save you. If you do not have that within yourselves, that which you do not have within will kill you."

Here, this author believes the word *have* no doubt should have been *are*. We should read it: "that which you are will save you." This simply is another way of saying that the discovery of your own God-Self is your salvation. My consciousness is what I am. It is my Self that does know it. It is my Self that does it because it is my Self that is it.

Jesus goes on to say, "If you bring forth that within yourselves, that which you have will save you. If you do not have that within yourselves, that which you do not have within you will kill you." Again, in the latter sentence, no doubt the word *have* should have been *are*. If you are not this within yourself and know it, that which you are not would be death itself—and death is nothingness. If you are not God, you are nothing. If the self you are is not God Itself being this Self, then you have no self; thus you *are* no self.

71. Jesus said, "I shall destroy this house and no one will be able to build it again."

107

Here again, the word *house* means body. He means, of course, that once we accept the body of Light, the body of Spirit, we no longer can perceive a body of matter. We no longer can accept the illusion that there is such a thing as <u>material substance in form</u>. This is not the destruction of the body; it is the realization of what the body really is.

72. A man said to him, "Tell my brethren to divide my father's possessions with me." He said to him, "Oh man, who made me a divider?" He turned to his disciples, and said to them, "I am not a divider, am I?"

Jesus knew there is one existence and this existence is God. He also knew that God being complete, He is <u>indivisible</u>, impartial abundance. God is Truth. <u>Truth cannot be divided</u>. It is impartial, indivisible, and impersonal. There is nothing in existence that can be divided. <u>Supply</u> is as impartial, as free, as the light or air. There is no lack. There is no division. To exist as the consciousness of this truth is to be aware of the impartiality, the equality, the indivisibility of the universe Itself, which is God. There is no lack in this consciousness. Actually, our inheritance is our God-conscious Identity.

73. Jesus said, "The harvest is indeed great, but the laborers are few; but beg the Lord to send

laborers into the harvest."

It is true that all perfection, complete perfection (the true harvest) is right here and right now, but there do not seem to be many, at the moment, that are ready to perceive it. They do not want to go all the way and still seem to prefer to hang back in the husks of twoness, of dualism. When Jesus speaks of laborers, about sending laborers into the harvest, he is not referring to teachers, authors, and the like. The word *laborers* should be interpreted as meaning sincere seekers of truth. It is not begging God to reveal more seekers for truth. It is God Itself more and more revealing Itself to be the very ones who seem to be seeking.

74. He said, "Lord, there are many around the cistern, but nobody in the cistern."

Yes, there do seem to be many who we may refer to as surface seekers. They seem perfectly content to go all the way around the field of dualism, but they seem unwilling to fully realize God is All and all is God.

75. Jesus said, "Many are standing at the door, but the solitary are the ones who will enter the bridal chamber."

The bridal chamber represents oneness, completeness. The bridal chamber represents a complete surrender of all fallacious beliefs—beliefs that there is an identity that of itself is something other than God; that it can do things separate from God; that it can know something besides God; that it can have something that is not God. It is in the complete surrender of the false, little self that the true and genuine Self is revealed; and it is in this revelation that the marriage, the oneness, is completely manifested and evidenced.

The bridal chamber also means pure, unblemished, undefiled consciousness. Solitary means the one who knows there is no other. Solitary means the one who knows its Self to be God as the only One, but also knows he is a specific identity. Yes, solitary means being the only One and knowing you are the only One.

76. Jesus said, "The kingdom of the Father is like a man, a merchant, who possessed merchandise and found a pearl. That merchant was prudent. He sold the merchandise and bought the one pearl for himself. Do you also seek for the treasure which fails not, which endures, there where no moth comes near to devour and where no worm destroys?"

That which seems to be man may possess many things of the so-called world, such as money, houses, friends, social lives, relatives, and loved ones, but all of this does not satisfy. There is no satisfaction until he recognizes his true Identity.

Pearl in this case means the genuine Identity. The discovery of the pearl is the discovery of the God-identity which is each of us.

When we discover our true God-identity, nothing of the so-called world exists for us. This includes our loved ones. At present they may appear to be "of the world," but eventually we realize they are specific God-identities also. They no longer exist as humans; they no longer exist as mortals. We discard all the material or mortal beliefs, our illusions of them as mortals, and see them as they are.

Again, finding the pearl is recognizing our genuine Identity. When we do this, we actually are recognizing the genuine Identity of all. We no longer are deluded. "He sold the merchandise"— in other words, he no longer acknowledges the delusion.

Then Jesus tells us to seek for the treasure that fails not. Seek to truly perceive, to know, that God, *supply* being the only one identified, does not change. God does not fail or disappoint us. Know that because God is the only supply, this supply cannot be depleted or fail. It matters not whether this supply is in the form of money, love, peace, joy, health, harmony, or life itself. This supply cannot fail and it cannot be depleted. This is what we are to seek, know, and understand. When we find this pearl, we discard all the beliefs and illusions of a divisible, temporal life of material persons, of mortal beings.

77. Jesus said, "I am the light that is above them all. I am the All. The All came forth from me and the All attained to me. Cleave a piece of wood; I am there. Lift up the stone, and you will find me there."

Jesus is saying, "The God that is my being is all there is. Therefore, I am the All; I am the only One." "I am the only One" can only be said when we are illumined and when we know it is not a human or mortal being trying to make some claim. In illumination we can say, "I am that which I am seeing; I am the All. Everything I see is my consciousness being that.

"The All came forth from me" is the All that I am. It is all my own consciousness. There is no other consciousness to be.

This next statement of Jesus is revealing the same truth. He is saying, "I am the substance of all form. Cleave a piece of wood, I am there; lift up the stone, and you will find me there." All is my own consciousness in form. It is all the *I* that I am.

78. Jesus said, "Why did you come out into the desert? To see a reed shaken by the wind? And to see a man clothed in soft garments? Your kings and your great ones are those who are clothed in soft garments, and they shall not be

able to know the truth."

It is apparent from this that Jesus did not want a following. He knew each was the same Consciousness that he was. Each is the same God-identity he was and is. He was asking, "Are you looking for an attractive man? Are you looking for a human being whom you consider to be kingly? Are you looking for a spiritual man in a body of matter? Are you looking for beauty in matter? Aren't you seeing that you are the same God identified that I am?"

In this case the word *kingly* represents those who think they have power of themselves. No one *has* power. There is only One, and that One *is* power. In illumination you know, I know, it is God being my being, God being your being, God being all there is of you, God being all there is of me. So how can anyone have power? It is God *being* power.

79. A woman from the multitude said to him, "Blessed is the womb which bore thee and the breasts which nourished thee." He said to her, "Blessed are those who have heard the word of the Father and have kept it in truth. For there will be the days when you will say, 'Blessed is the womb which has not conceived and the breasts which have not suckled.' "

Jesus knew this woman was seeing him as a man born of a woman. She was not yet ready to hear there is no birth. When he said, "Blessed are those who have heard the word," the "word" is truth. The word is the truth that there is no birth. And Jesus was saying, "You will perceive there is no creation and no creator." He goes on to say that there will come a time when you will realize there is no birth, when you will awaken and be fully and completely awake.

80. Jesus said, "Whoever has known the world has found the body, and whoever has found the body, of him the world is not worthy."

Actually, there is one body, and this body is God Itself as the body of the universe. The allness of God is the body that is God, but there is nothing outside the body. When we really realize what the world is, what the universe is, then we begin to realize what the body is. It is in this perception that the universal essence, which is the essence of the body, is realized. This is the body of your Identity. The body that is your Identity is seen to be the perfect, active, universal body of Light, and you are experiencing your perfect, active, universal body as your active Identity.

81. Jesus said, "Let him who has become rich become king, and let him who has power renounce it."

Let him who realizes what he is, who has discovered his identity, know that he is the king of his kingdom; but let him who misperceives that, as a human being or someone other than God, renounce the power he believes he has. In other words, the human being is nothing and has no power.

82. Jesus said, "Whoever is near to me is near to the fire, and whoever is far from me is far from the kingdom."

Jesus means that whoever is near, or close to the realization that he himself is the Christ, is already enlightened. The fire means light, so if we are far from the fire, we are far from awakening to the fact that our consciousness is our kingdom.

83. Jesus said, "The images are manifest to man, and the Light which is within them is hidden in the Image of the Light of the Father. He will manifest himself, and His Image is concealed by His Light."

All of us know that often in illumination we have no awareness of having a body. Sometimes we do, but more often we don't. This is because the Light in illumination is so intense, beautiful, and bright. The Light conceals what seems to be the outline of the form of the body. This does not mean we lose awareness of the fact we are a body.

It's just that the Light is so great it conceals it. However, if there is the misperception or misconception that there is a body of matter here, this apparent body of matter can seem to conceal the body of Light that *is* here right now.

84. Jesus said, "When you see your likeness, you rejoice. But when you see your images which came into existence before you, which neither die nor are manifested, how much you will bear!"

It is true that when we begin along this path and are aware of a better and more perfect body of matter we rejoice; but it is almost more than we can bear when, as illumined beings, we see this body as it actually is—a body of Light. When Jesus speaks of "your images which came into existence before you," he's speaking of the body that has always existed, even before you seemed to be born.

85. Jesus said, "Adam came into existence from a great power and a great wealth, and yet he did not become worthy of you. For if he had been worthy, he would not have tasted death."

Yes, Jesus admits here that there does seem to be the mass mesmerism called birth, but he also says that actually, right now, we are at the point where we know there is no birth. Then he says that if Adam had realized the foregoing, he would not even have seemed to die. And yes, we do realize we do not have to seem to die.

86. Jesus said, "The foxes have their holes and the birds have their nest, but the son of man has no place to lay his head and rest."

What is meant here is that there is no rest or peace in the belief that we live in a material world in a body of matter.

87. Jesus said, "Wretched is the body which depends upon a body, and wretched is the soul which depends upon these two."

Wretched is the belief that there is a dependence upon a body of matter for life, for peace, for harmony. The word *soul* here means the so-called human sense of life. What he is saying is, "Wretched is that illusory sense which calls itself soul, or material sense, depending upon a mortal body for its existence, continuity, and for its life. Wretched are you if you depend upon a human soul in a body of matter."

88. Jesus said, "The angels and prophets will come to you, and they will give you what is yours. And you, too, give to them what is in your hands, and say to yourselves, 'On which day will they come and receive what is theirs?' "

Jesus here is speaking of those who write or "teach" this truth. If they really see and know, they realize they are not giving this truth to anyone apart from themselves. They realize the one before them is the very same Consciousness they are.

89. Jesus said, "Why do you wash the outside of the cup? Do you not understand that he who made the inside is also he who made the outside?"

There is no inside and there is no outside. The inside and outside are both the same essence. There is no space and there is no time. There is only infinity. There is only eternity. There is only now, and there is only here.

90. Jesus said, "Come to me, for easy is my yoke and my lordship is gentle, and you shall find repose for yourselves."

This is another way of saying that love is always gentle, never harsh. Love is always compassionate.

91. They said to him, "Tell us who thou art so that we may believe in thee." He said to them, "You test the face of the sky and of the earth, and him who is before your face you have not known, and you do not know to test this moment."

Jesus tells them that if they knew what constitutes the sky and the earth, they would know what constitutes the one standing before them.

92. Jesus said, "Seek and you will find, but those things which you asked me in those days, I did

not tell you then; now I desire to tell them, but you do not inquire after them."

Jesus is telling them that he knew them before they seemed to be born. Then he didn't have to tell them anything because they were awake. Now they seem to be buried in matter and asleep. They are not even awake enough to ask Jesus about what is really true.

(Verses 93 through 96—See Addendum)

97. Jesus said, "The kingdom of the Father is like a woman who was carrying a jar full of meal. While she was walking on a distant road, the handle of the jar broke. The meal streamed out behind her on the road. She did not know it; she had noticed no accident. After she came into her house, she put the jar down and found it empty."

This is a beautiful and glorious illustration of what happens with us. Sometimes our burden does seem to be heavy, and we may seem to carry it for a very long, long time. Many times it may seem our burden is getting even heavier, darker, more massive and forbidding, more threatening and frightening—but we do arrive at the point when we put the jar down and awaken. We discover our burden was slowly leaking away as was the meal in the jar. What really was happening was that our burden was being dissipated, dispersed, and dispensed with. We seemed in our darker moments not even to realize that our burden was actually disappearing. When we awakened, we realized we never really had the burden; we never carried it and it never existed.

98. Jesus said, "The kingdom of the Father is like a man who wished to kill a powerful man. He drew the sword in his own house, and he stuck it into the wall in order to know whether his hand would carry through; then he slew the powerful man."

It does seem we have to eliminate, disperse, or dispense with a power other than God, another being apart from God. To do this does seem to be a test of our spiritual strength. We do thrust out, as if with a sword, to dispense with the seeming power other than God. It is with this test of our strength, our conviction that we are the strength, which enables us to carry through. We are then seeing through what appears to be another power.

99. The disciples said to him, "Thy brethren and thy mother are standing outside." He said to them, "Those here who do the will of my Father, they are my brethren and my mother; these are they who shall enter the kingdom of my Father."

Jesus is again referring to the fact that there is no birth, no human relations, and there are no human mothers or fathers, and whoever perceives this is already in the kingdom of God. He already is the Consciousness which is the kingdom of God.

100. They showed Jesus a gold coin and said to him, "Caesar's men ask taxes from us." He said to them, "Give the things of Caesar to Caesar, give the things of God to God, and give me what is mine."

Of course, the secret here is when he says, "Give me what is mine." This means to live a normal life. Go about your business and do all the things that are necessary for you to do, but maintain your consciousness that you are the Christ Itself. You are the Christ-Self being Itself.

101. Jesus said, "Whoever does not hate his father and his mother in my way will not be able to be a disciple to me, and whoever does not love his father and his mother in my way will not be able to be a disciple to me. For my mother [...], but my true Mother gave me life."

This has nothing to do with hating, of course. Actually, what he is saying is that those who do not realize they have neither a human mother nor a human father cannot possibly understand what he is saying. Love those who seem to be your human mother and father, knowing full well they are the same Consciousness you are. Then Jesus goes on to say, "My true Mother gave me life." "My true Mother" is my own being, my own God-Consciousness.

(Verses 102, 103 and beginning of 104—See Addendum)

104. "But when the bridegroom comes out of the bridal chamber, then let them fast and let them pray."

When we seem to depart from our realization that there is one God and this God is all there is, then we have to try to awaken and fast from the things of the so-called material world.

(Verse 105—See Addendum)

106. Jesus said, "When you make the two one, you shall become sons of Man, and when you say, 'Mountain, be moved,' it will be moved."

Jesus again and again called himself the son of Man, and you notice the word *Man* is always capitalized. When you realize there aren't two but only one, you will realize that the Father and the Son are this One. It is in this realization that there is the power to move mountains.

(Verses 107 through 113—See Addendum)

114. Simon Peter said to them, "Let Mary go out from among us, because women are not worthy of the Life." Jesus said, "I shall lead her so that I

will make her male, that she too may become a living spirit resembling you males. For every woman who makes herself male will enter the kingdom of heaven."

This perhaps is the greatest revelation of all of the one hundred and fourteen sayings of Jesus in this volume.

The species called man is but one aspect of God. Male and female are distinct aspects of this species. The function of the male is that distinct function, as the function of the female is that distinct function. However, this has nothing to do with bodies of matter.

In this revelation, the male and the female are the same. Each is alive and each is Life identified. Each is conscious because each is the same Consciousness. Each is intelligent because each is the same Mind. Each is loving because each is the same Love. Neither of them can usurp the identity or the function of the other. Yet it is the same God identified as both the female and the male.

Addendum

Friends, there is infinitely more in the foregoing and following sayings of Jesus Christ. Read them over and over and discover the joy of your own revelations within your own consciousness.

93. Jesus said, "Give not what is holy to the dogs, lest they cast it on the dung-heap. Throw not the pearls to the swine, lest they make it [...]."

94. Jesus said, "Whoever seeks will find and whoever knocks, it will be opened to him."

95. Jesus said, "If you have money, do not lend at interest, but give it to him from whom you will not receive it back."

96. Jesus said, "The kingdom of the Father is like a woman who has taken a little leaven, hid it in dough, and made it into large loaves of bread. Whoever has ears, let him hear."

102. Jesus said, "Woe to them, the Pharisees, for they are like a dog sleeping in the manger of oxen, for neither does he eat nor does he allow the oxen to eat."

103. Jesus said, "Blessed is the man who knows in which part of the night the robbers will come

in, so that he will rise and collect his estate and gird up his loins before they come in."

104. They said to him, "Come and let us pray today and let us fast." Jesus said, "Which then is the sin that I have committed, or in what have I been vanquished?"

105. Jesus said, "Whoever knows father and mother shall be called the son of a harlot."

107. Jesus said, "The kingdom is like a shepherd who had a hundred sheep. One of them went astray, which was the largest. He left behind ninety-nine and sought for the one until he found it. Having tired himself out, he said to the sheep, 'I love thee more than the ninety-nine.'"

108. Jesus said, "Whoever drinks from my mouth shall become as I am, and I myself will become he, and the hidden things shall be revealed to him."

109. Jesus said, "The kingdom is like a man who had a treasure hidden in his field without knowing it. And after he died, he left it to his son. The son did not know about it. He accepted that field and sold it. And he who bought it, while he was plowing found the treasure. He began to lend money to whomever he wished."

110. Jesus said, "Whoever has found the world and become rich, let him deny the world."

111. Jesus said, "The heavens will be rolled up and the earth in your presence, and he who lives from the Living One shall see neither death nor fear" because Jesus says. "Whoever finds himself, of him the world is not worthy."

112. Jesus said, "Woe to the flesh which depends upon the soul; woe is the soul which depends upon the flesh."

113. His disciples said to him, "When will the kingdom come?" Jesus said, "It will not come by expectation. They will not say, 'See, here,' or 'See, there.' Rather the kingdom of the Father is spread upon the earth, and men do not see it."

About the Author

During early childhood, Marie S. Watts began questioning: "Why am I? What am I? Where is God? What is God?"

After experiencing her first illumination at seven years of age, her hunger for the answers to these questions became intensified. Although she became a concert pianist, her search for the answers continued, leading her to study all religions, including those of the East.

Finally, ill and unsatisfied, she gave up her profession of music, discarded all books of ancient and modern religions, kept only the Bible, and went into virtual seclusion from the world for some eight years. It was out of the revelations and illuminations she experienced during those years, revelations that were sometimes the very opposite of what she had hitherto believed, that her own healing was realized and that the book, *The Ultimate*, came.

During all the previous years, she had been active in helping others. After 1957, she devoted herself exclusively to the continuance of this healing work and to lecturing and teaching. Revelations continually came to her and these have been set forth in this and every book.

To all seekers for Light, for Truth, for God, for an understanding of their own true Being, each of her books will serve as a revolutionary guide.

38 no death experience at all [7/1/2016]; top 117
51 no material procreation
104 The cornerstone: There is no birth. [10/5/2019]